SHOOTING
IN THE DARK

Tales of Coaching and Leadership

February 20, 1999

With admiration and gratefulness to the 1st Alison in my life!

Jim Thompson

Jim Thompson

Warde Publishers
Portola Valley, California

Warde Publishers, Inc.
3000 Alpine Road
Portola Valley, CA 94028
(800) 699-2733

The excerpt on pages 126–128, from an article by Geoff Lepper which appeared in the Palo Alto Daily News, is reprinted with permission from the Palo Alto Daily News.

The poem on page 70, "Normal Day" by Mary Jean Irion, is reprinted with permission from the author.

Publisher's Cataloging-in-Publication Data
Thompson, Jim, 1949–
    Shooting in the dark : tales of coaching and leadership /
Jim Thompson. —1st ed.
    p. cm.
    Includes bibliographical references and index.
    ISBN: 1-886346-04-6

    1. Coaching (Athletics)   2. Thompson, Jim, 1949–
3. Basketball for girls—Coaching.   4. Leadership.   Coaches
(Athletics)   I. Title.
GV711.T46 1998   796.07'7

                                         QBI98–566

Contents

Foreword

by Phil Jackson
Head Coach, Chicago Bulls

Several years ago, Rich Kelley, a former colleague of mine, sent me a loose-leafed manuscript written by a friend who was his instructor at the Stanford School of Business. Rich called to tell me about Jim Thompson and the book, *Positive Coaching*. I liked the book and volunteered to write a positive critique for the cover. I have used some of Jim Thompson's methods in my efforts to become a better coach. So it is that Jim and I became acquaintances united by the common thread of having survived growing up in North Dakota. This summer I received another of Jim's explorations into the world of coaching, *Shooting in the Dark: Tales of Coaching and Leadership*. It is an even better aid to coaching.

In the effort to lead athletes, coaches sometimes turn to the tried and true measures applied to them when they were young athletes. In looking back, they must honestly decide to use those methods that were useful and positive, and reject what wasn't beneficial. In my lifetime, there has been a great change in the authoritarian figure of the "coach," which was surely the next step behind the father figure (there were few, if any, women coaches at that time). As we grew up, the Woody Hayeses and Vince Lombardis became obsolete and new models were needed to replace the militaristic-athletic coach/leader. Ground has been broken in the 1990's with the creation of a new coaching model. It is no longer just the coach who yells, "My way or the highway" who gets respect and effort from his players, and is not seen as a wimp. This new type of coach is one whose leadership is trusted because he shares it with his players.

Shooting in the Dark brings those ideals into focus as the reader travels uncharted highways with Jim in his effort to learn by feel how all this works. It is fun to go with Jim and his team into the dark as we travel a path he is searching to find on his own.

When I think of the variety of coaching styles I have experienced in my lifetime, it makes me wonder how I got where I am. I had two Marines for coaches—one was at Iwo Jima, both believed in driving a player toward personal breakdown. I had a Lutheran Deacon who, after a high school championship, decided to leave coaching and become a state politician. Most of these men were influenced by Knute Rockne and men of iron-fisted rule, who believed that authority and discipline were the keys to winning teams. They may have been right for their time because World War II and subsequent wars in Korea and Vietnam demanded that young men fight in battle without questioning the objectives. But we have changed as a society. Today the participants aren't ready to charge into battle against insurmountable odds. We are in a user-friendly era, and, as a result, coaching has taken on a different persuasion. The effort required, however, is the same. The sacrifice might still be as much and the talent is surely greater as each generation of athletes surpasses the previous generation.

You will find Jim's tactics useful at many levels of leadership or teaching. Jim ends each chapter with what he calls Take-Aways, key points that are emphasized in one-sentence summaries. The Take-Aways make *Shooting in the Dark* very easy to use as a quick review before you go into your classroom or gym to teach.

Learning how to meter out the emotion of the moment so as to be able to succeed over the long term is something every coach struggles with. Jim has included check points in diary-type entries that give the reader an opportunity to see how he felt at key moments and then through reflection how that impulse worked out in his coaching.

It is important for every coach to remember that what you are doing is totally unique to the group you have assembled. Each person brings a different characteristic to the whole and because of that there are no concrete rules that govern situations. A coach has to be able to flow with the group. That means not always forcing your will upon the team or classroom.

Perhaps this is what Jim Thompson's writings will teach you the most— you have the opportunity to lead in a relaxed state of awareness, so that situations that present new approaches can be accepted with a "soft adaptable mind." Coaches should keep seeking solutions that bring the group to a new pinnacle experience. That's what hooks us on this life of coaching and teaching and it's what keeps players joyful about playing.

Preface

A thing is incredible, if ever, only after it is told—returned to the world it came out of.

—Eudora Welty

The "tales" in this book arise largely from my two years coaching the Fremont High School girls basketball team in Sunnyvale, California, beginning in May 1994. When, almost exactly two years later, the coaching job dematerialized quite as surprisingly as it had appeared, I felt a lack of closure on the experience. I had so many reactions, insights, stories, and feelings that were just bursting to be told.

About that time, the Stanford Graduate School of Business (GSB) changed e-mail systems to one called "Eudora," after Eudora Welty, a writer I had heard great things about but whose work I had never read. The changeover seemed like a signal that I should read Ms. Welty, since the fellow who designed Eudora thought enough of her to name his creation for her. I bought a book of her short stories and came across one called "No Place for You, My Love," in which I found the sentence at the top of this page. I realized she articulated the truth about my experiences of the last two years. The many exciting and wonderous tales of the Women Warriors of Fremont High School would be incredible only if I wrote about them to sustain them against the memory ravages of time. As I shared some of them with friends, I began to realize that there might be a book here that others would find interesting.

I have always had a difficult time compartmentalizing. My coaching experience influences my family life, which influences my work life, which influences my coaching, etc., etc. My coaching experience at Fremont High School was heavily shaped by coinciding with a course I was co-teaching at the GSB called Learning to Lead.

Like coaching the Women Warriors, Learning to Lead was a labor of love. A few years earlier I had been involved with a faculty task force charged with looking at what the GSB should be doing in the area of leadership education. I had a lot of thoughts about leadership development, having served as Director of the GSB's Public Management Program (PMP) since 1987. From the day I was hired my goal was to reconfigure the PMP into a student-driven leadership development program to prepare our MBA students for leadership in public service.

Over the next few years our students engaged in social entrepreneurship in a way that has transformed the GSB, and left a legacy of organizational responses to local and international social problems. In 1991–92 Stanford MBA students raised nearly a half-million dollars and created an I Have a Dream chapter to guarantee college funds for elementary school kids at Flood School in the nearby Ravenswood City School District. In 1993–94 another group created an organization called Start Up, which trains would-be entrepreneurs in East Palo Alto on business basics and provides seed loans when the entrepreneurs are ready to start their businesses.* A third group, in 1995–96, created an organization called MBAid (MBAs in Development) to send business students to developing countries to contribute their business skills to non-governmental organizations in places like Brazil, Vietnam, South Africa and Cameroon.

I was gratified in 1992 when *U.S. News* named the PMP the top non-profit business-management program in the nation, but I also thought there were opportunities to go further. Thus when asked to be part of the

---

*Early in 1998, Start Up was recognized by the President's Initiative on Race as an example of a "best practice."

GSB's leadership task force, I jumped at the chance, even though I already had a full plate of responsibilities.

John Gardner, whose wisdom inspired Learning to Lead, has said that professional schools should be bridges between the world of ideas and what he calls the "untidy world of action." At any academic professional school, there is tension between faculty with a long-term, analytical, research-oriented view and impatient students wanting to know how what they are being taught in the classroom relates to the demanding jobs they will begin when they graduate. At its best, the Stanford GSB maintains a dynamic tension between faculty and students that results in some incredible exchanges of insight. Faculty challenge students to look beyond "best current practices" and anecdotes to the underlying principles involved. Students challenge faculty to demonstrate that their research has relevance to the real world. It is an amazingly stimulating environment.

While it is important to bridge the idea/action gap in any course in a professional school, a course in leadership practically cries out for it. Leadership is a performing art, and the best way to get better at it is to practice it *while* learning about it. So, we required students in the class to have a "practice arena"—usually a leadership role in a student activity—in which they would have both the opportunity and the responsibility to try out the ideas in the course.

Learning to Lead was several years in development. Shortly after Jerry Porras, David Bradford, Debra Meyerson, and I began teaching it, the coaching job at Fremont High School dropped into my lap. Learning to Lead constituted a great opportunity to learn from my colleagues and students, as well as from the incredible array of dynamic leaders we had as guests in the course. Orchestra conductors, CEOs, athletic coaches, community organizers, nonprofit and government leaders, venture capitalists, you name it—we had some of the top people in the *world* speak in our course. I immediately grasped that coaching a basketball team could be *my* practice arena in which I too could try out the ideas that bubbled up in the classroom.

Good for the goose, good for the gander. My own learning (and teaching) would be enhanced just as much as that of the students if I made continual, conscious, and conscientious efforts to *use* what I heard and read and taught. And it never seemed forced. I tend to see much of the world as a basketball game and basketball as a metaphor for life. (I subscribe to Phil Jackson's maxim from his book *Sacred Hoops*: "Not only is there more to life than basketball, there's a lot more to basketball than basketball.") Much of the wisdom shared in the class-room seemed tailor-made for the basketball court, just as the results (for good and ill) of my attempts to implement that wisdom with the Women Warriors seemed to have ramifications for organizational life far beyond the athletic world.

One other source for this book deserves mention. I have been neither a compulsive nor conscientious journal writer during my life, but I have found that I tend to write more when I am troubled or challenged. Several years ago I began following the advice of Julia Cameron in her remarkable book *The Artist's Way* to write daily "morning pages." Although my efforts were sporadic rather than comprehensive, when I went back to check, I found many more journal entries during that period than I would have guessed. And many of them were relevant and on point to what became this book.

The journal entries assumed greater importance because I was torn between a book in chronological narrative form and one organized around topics of interest to coaches and other leaders. I finally con-cluded that a narrative was less effective as a vehicle for what I wanted to say in the book. Yet I continued to fret about the dramatic *story* of this particular team of girls and how that story played out on the basketball floor.

As I reviewed my journal the idea came to me that perhaps I could eat my cake and still have it.* Through judicious use of journal entries and interludes I found I could interweave the how-to (and how-*not*-to) parts of the book with a narrative that might convey some of the excite-ment I experienced coaching this team during those two years.

The interludes are chronological and catch the reader up on the ex-perience of the team throughout the two years. The journal entries do not follow a chronology. Instead I have tried to place them in the chapter

---

*I have always felt that the traditional version of this cliché didn't make sense—"have your cake and eat it too." Of course you can only eat your cake after you have it. It was only after I reversed it during my college years that it finally made sense to me—you eat it but you still have it afterwards. Needless to say I was chagrined to discover that one of the clues that revealed the identity of the alleged Unabomber to his brother was the phrase "eat your cake and have it too" in the Unabomber's manifesto. His brother recognized the phrase and *be-lieved* that no one else said it that way, and went to the FBI with his suspicions.

in which they have something to add to the topic at hand. They tend to spotlight my inner thoughts and feelings as I struggled with the challenge of coaching.

A note about the title. "Shooting in the Dark" comes from a special moment in the lives of the Women Warriors that occurred early one summer morning in 1995 and is described in, and is also the title of, Chapter 6. But in another sense entirely, it is an apt metaphor for the ambiguous, messy, and mind-boggling task of trying to lead. Jim Clawson, at the Darden Business School at the University of Virginia, uses the term *edge abrasion* to describe the process of wearing down that leaders face by so often being out on the edge of the boat peering into the distance, trying to figure out which way to go. I like to describe technology as the process of taking something that took one or more really-smart people a long time to figure out and turning it into something that any boob can easily do. Well, there is, as yet, no technology of leadership that allows any boob to lead successfully. Any leader worth his salt is shooting in the dark any time he "goes beyond the map," which should be often.

Certainly *Shooting in the Dark* falls far short of providing a technology of leadership. However, I do feel, having lived and then written this book, that *now* I just may be ready to become a pretty decent coach. In any event, it has been—both the doing and the writing—a challenging effort entirely entwined with enjoyment. I hope you will find it enjoyable and helpful to whatever leadership challenge you find yourself confronting.

Jim Thompson
May, 1998

Acknowledgments

Appreciation is the glue that binds people and organizations together. I have so much appreciation to express to so many people connected to the creation of *Shooting in the Dark*. I often think of ifs that might not have become thens.

If Bill Stokes hadn't gotten me thinking. If Phil Kelly hadn't encourage me to apply for the coaching job. If Jerry Porras hadn't invited me to join the LTL team. If Sandra Hietala hadn't supported my wild dream. If Lori Cox hadn't shown up at a Cupertino Hoops coaches meeting. If the Women Warriors hadn't responded to and gone well beyond my coaching. If Rich Kelley hadn't introduced me to Jake Warde. You get the idea. Here's a partial list of those I appreciate.

First and foremost are the Fremont Varsity Women Warriors themselves: Lillian Ito, Shelly Savage, Karen Ahrens, Amalia Castelino, Shauna Harrison, Sheila Hess, Colleen Smith, Haruka Soejima, Chi Tran, Jenny White, and Natalie Woo. It would be hard for any coach to be unsuccessful with such a great bunch of young women. They taught me a lot and made coaching so much fun. They were winners in basketball and they will be winners in life.

I learned from three outstanding assistant coaches: Lori Cox, who dropped out of the sky to teach me about basketball and intensity; Leticia Cruz Guzman, with her infectious enthusiasm, now on her way to becoming a great teacher; and Annie van den Toorn, who may have to choose between being a great coach and a business tycoon—either are attainable. Any coach would be delighted to have them as part of a leadership team.

Phil Kelly, Fremont High School athletic director and emeritus basketball coach extraordinaire, took a chance on a rookie coach. Lots of other great people in and around Fremont High School had hands in this book: John Mackey, Pat Lawson, Bob Stahl, Debbie Blasquez, Jason Crutchfield, Alma Barajas, Tara McDonough, Kim Johnson, Shannon

Lynas, George Guinden, Charlotte Salvacion, Miguel Castillo, Dieu Vuong, John White, Georgi White, Carol Smith, Phil Smith, Kerry Smith, and Judd Smith, who was unwavering in his support and good humor. A special word of appreciation is due Cyp Sena whose death left a gentle void at Fremont High School. Jeff Myers, videographer and track coach, I still owe you a dinner!

Many friends gave me valuable feedback: Andrew Oser, Jo Felsenthal, Tom Copeland, Richard Close, Marisha Chamberlain, Ann Doherty, Tim Rumsey, Katie Peuvrelle, Ivy Millman, Jim Richardson, and Drew Petersen. Rich Kelley was a source of regular encouragement, content and grammatical improvements, and basketball strategy advice. Bill Stokes remains a friend in spite of what he got me into. This book wouldn't have happened without his meddling.

My colleagues in Learning to Lead, Jerry Porras, David Bradford, and Debra Meyerson modeled leadership and great teaching every day in class. It was the equivalent of an old style apprenticeship and I am grateful to have been their apprentice. Others at the Stanford Graduate School of Business provided encouragement and support: John Gardner, David Brady, Jim Patell, George Parker, Bill Barnett, Charles O'Reilly, Jeff Pfeffer, Jim March, Tim Wei, Uta Kremer, Marie Mookini, Sib Farrell, Rosa Hamilton, Heather Ramirez, Barbara Kent, Kathy Davis, Kim Smith, and Lauren Dutton. Michael Ray's Creativity in Business course helped jump-start this book. Alison Carlson, who has become the ace of the Public and Global Management Programs, gave me many insights that improved the book. Gene Webb, taken well before his time, lingers in my memory with his wit and wisdom.

The many Stanford MBA students who dared to take Learning to Lead taught me much about teaching, coaching and leadership. Two of them, Juliet Thompson Hochman and Eric Reveno, shared their extraordinary expertise with the Women Warriors. They combine the best aspects of sports and business. Many others made suggestions and gave encouragement at key moments: Craig Spence, Ivor Frischknecht, Brent Leland, Ted DesMaisons, Vân Ton, Fran Sachs, and Jay Stokes in particular.

Jake Warde is the entrepreneurial brains behind Warde Publishers, a future major publishing house! When I hear of the horrors that so many writers experience in this brave new world of publishing, I am even more grateful that Rich Kelley got us together.

I'm indebted to many, many coaches. Mike Dunlap gave me advice in December 1994 that was invaluable in turning around a season that seemed to be heading for the dumpster. Tara VanDerveer shared insights worth their weight in gold. Dave Crawford took me under his wing and reduced the number of Rookie Moves I made. Ron Rossi provided a sounding board many times—some day we'll get the chance to coach together! Jeff McKay, a coaching guru and "teacher of athletes," has been a lifelong friend and coaching colleague for the past five years. I enjoyed matching wits with fellow high school coaches Ernie Dossa, Ron Ingram, Dave Blasquez, Debbie Gudis, Rich Prsha, Ken Kline, David Lee, Jeff Lamb, Brian Harrigan, Jeff Frost, Bret Yeilding, and Doug Lee, among others. Phil Jackson has been an inspiration—demonstrating both that it is possible to succeed at the highest levels as a professional coach without sacrificing principles and that being from North Dakota is an asset.

Others I've never met did their part. Julia Cameron's morning pages helped me keep going and provided raw material for this book. John Fogerty and Creedence Clearwater Revival gave us a boost at Saturday morning practices and games. I agree with Jenny. It's hard to believe so many great basketball songs came from one group. I appreciate Mary Jean Irion for giving permission to use her powerful "Normal Day." I don't know if it's a poem either, but it is everything a great poem should be.

My family is as good an example of God's grace as I could imagine. My stepfather, Orville, demonstrated great courage during several traumatic illnesses before passing away just before this book was published. He is missed. My father, Bill, remains one of the most optimistic people in the world. My son, Gabriel, is now a man of intellect and compassion (and according to his grandmother, the best writer in the family!). My buttons bust when I think of him. My wife, Sandra, failed miserably when I begged her to talk me out of this. Everything good in my life is connected with her! She remains my spiritual guide.

Finally, I dedicate this book to the first woman warrior in my life, my mother, Marjorie Eileen Lorraine Score Thompson Bjerkager, whose determination to recover from a stroke and heart surgery has been an inspiration. This time I am determined to spell all her names correctly! Although I tease her that it's a wonder I turned out as well as I did, I could hardly have gone wrong with her as my mother.

Talk Me Out of This!

God made the world round so we shouldn't be able to look too far down the road.

— Isak Dineson, **Out of Africa**

As with many life-altering events, there was no warning.

It was a winter Saturday morning like many others. As manager of coaches for Cupertino Hoops, a youth basketball league I had helped to found several years before, I walked into the gymnasium at Fremont High School in Sunnyvale, California, as I had done many times before. There I saw my old friend, Bill Stokes, who was the league's referees manager. Bill loved to referee, so whenever a scheduled ref failed to show up Bill took his place. This particular day, Bill was in luck because one of the refs had had car trouble. At half-time he came over to say hello. So far, pretty innocent. Then he dropped the hammer. "I was talking with Sandy Coolidge the other day and we both agreed that you aren't contributing as much to Cupertino Hoops as you could be."

Now these were provocative words. I was already feeling stretched by my job, some writing projects, and family responsibilities, as well as the various tasks I had agreed to perform for Cupertino Hoops. After every recent basketball season I had felt burned out and ready to resign from the board of directors but by the time September came around I signed up again, partly because I liked the people involved so much. And then, when I went to the season-beginning Jamboree in December, it was so great to see all of those kids in their new uniforms having a great time playing basketball that it all seemed worth it. So Bill's criticism rankled.

However, one thing I have learned over the years is that it is worth the effort to try really hard to see criticism as a gift. If someone gives you a gift for your birthday and it doesn't fit or you don't like it, you don't tell them that. You thank them for it and wait until later to examine it privately, to see if you want to keep it, or put it in the attic and forget about it.

With the gift of criticism, I try to say something like "Thanks for sharing that. You might be right. I'll consider it." Then, metaphorically, I put it in my shirt pocket and think about it later when I am alone and feeling less threatened to see if it fits and is something I want to use to change my behavior. So, quashing my annoyance and summoning up my will power, I said to Bill, "What do you mean?" in as polite a tone as I could muster.

"Well, both Sandy and I agree that the best experience our daughters have had with basketball was when you coached them on a Cupertino Hoops team several years ago. We think it's a waste for you to be doing only administrative work for the league. You should be coaching."

Now that kind of criticism I can handle!

It turned out that Bill's daughter, who started on her high school varsity basketall team as a freshman, was having a less-than-ideal experience as a sophomore. As we continued the conversation after the game, Bill had an idea. "Would you be interested in being an assistant coach for Katie's team? As an assistant you wouldn't have to always be at practice so there'd be less pressure."

Although I didn't let on just then, I was intrigued. I had often thought about coaching high school basketball—especially after writing a book on coaching youth sports (*Positive Coaching: Building Character and Self-Esteem Through Sports*)—and I had also always wanted a daughter to go with my wonderful son. So the idea of coaching a girls' basketball team was interesting. And being an assistant was a low-risk way to get started.

I told Bill I would think about it and get back to him. Over the next few days, the more I thought about the pros and cons I began to realize that, under the right circumstances, I would love to do it. I called him to say that if the head coach would listen to some of my ideas, I'd be interested in giving it a try. I didn't want to work with someone who would resent me or disregard all my input.

Bill agreed to give a copy of *Positive Coaching* to the coach and talk to him to see if he would be interested in such a partnership. He called me a few days later to say that he had talked to the coach, who was open to the idea. The next step was to get together and assess whether we could work together in a productive fashion. Bill agreed to set that up.

A few days later Bill called. "Jim, guess what?" It turned out that the coach in question was no longer the coach. It seemed some of the parents were unhappy with his performance and were not shy about sharing their feelings with the principal. The bottom line: the head coaching position was open! Did I want to apply for it?

Intellectually, I was afraid that I didn't know enough about high school basketball to be a head coach right out of the box. There is a lot of security in being the second banana when beginning a new venture.

Emotionally, I was hooked. There was really no way I was *not* going to apply for the job. And besides, applying for it didn't mean that I would have to do it. I might not get the job. And if I were offered it, I wouldn't have to take it. After a couple more days of reflection to make sure that this crazy idea wasn't going to go away, I called Bill to say that I would indeed apply for the job, and since he had gotten me into this, I wanted a favor from him. I asked him to call the school principal and put in a good word for me to keep him from going ahead and filling the job before I got a decent shot at it. He agreed.

I got my application in and waited. A few days later a call came from Phil Kelly, the athletic director at Fremont High School, someone I had known and respected both as a coach and a person for many years. He said, "Jim, I'm really disappointed in you." My first thought was that some Cupertino Hoops coach had done something awful to the Fremont High School gym last week.

"I understand you applied for the girls basketball job over at School X. I'm upset that you didn't apply here at Fremont."

"Well, gee, Phil, I didn't know there was an opening at Fremont." Did I want to be considered for it? Yes, I did! After all, I was emotionally committed to coaching now and I might not get the job at School X. According to the rumor mill, the boys coach at School X had a favorite candidate for the job, so the interview process might just be a formality with the decision already having been made.

A few days later Phil called to set up an interview. The interview committee consisted of the vice principal, the two athletic directors, Pat Lawson and Phil, the retiring coach, John Mackey, and three of the players. The latter, I thought, was a really good sign. Involving the players—a senior named Lillian and two juniors, Colleen and Jenny—in a decision that affected them so greatly was the kind of thing that Phil would do.

I don't remember too much about the interview, having been in a bit of a daze. The vice principal, Cyp Sena, asked me how long I was willing to commit to the job if hired, given that coaching changes were disruptive to the players (an ironic question, it would turn out). I responded as honestly as I could that I wouldn't guarantee anything because, with my job and other responsibilities, I might find it was too difficult to do justice to coaching, in which case I would only do it for one year. However, I was pretty sure I could handle it, that I would enjoy it, and so I might well be doing it the rest of my life. Then I went home to wait.

Journal Entry—April 12, 1994

Bill Walsh spoke in Learning to Lead today. He spoke mostly about his time with the 49ers and a bit about his decision to return to Stanford to coach. It is clear that a major secret of his success was preparation. He told a riveting story about a 1975 playoff game against the Oakland Raiders in which the Cincinnati Bengals, whose offense he ran, recovered a fumble in Raiders' territory with time running out, trailing by three points. He described in graphic terms his "interaction" with the Raiders fans. In the Oakland Coliseum the home town fans knew the location of the opposing coaches' box from which the offensive coordinator called plays. The box was glassed in but there was an opening in the glass. In those last few minutes, the Oakland fans began pelting Walsh with bananas and garbage! Needing to gain only a few yards to get within range of a tying field goal, Walsh says he called the four worst plays of his life and the Bengals lost the game and the chance to advance to the Super Bowl.

Walsh vowed after that that he would never again in his life have to be "creative under pressure." When he became the head coach of the 49ers, they drilled every conceivable last-second situation so that the team knew what to do because they had done it so many times before. Sure enough, in a 1987 game, this time *against* the Bengals, the 49ers got the ball on the Bengals' 25-yard line with two seconds left on the clock, trailing 26–20.

Walsh painted a great picture of the Cincinnati stadium. The Bengal fans were ecstatic, certain that their team had beaten the 49ers. A friend of Walsh's was in the men's room about this time and the Bengals fans were laughing and yukking it up. But someone had a transistor radio tuned to the game and for just a moment there was a gap in the cheering long enough for everyone to hear the announcer saying "Montana drops back . . ." The restroom got very quiet as they listened to the radio description of Joe Monanta's winning touchdown pass to Jerry Rice. Walsh said he wouldn't have even had to call the play, so well prepared were the 49ers for just such a situation.

Near the end of Walsh's speech, one of the students asked if he thought his coaching experience would allow him to run a major corporation successfully. He said "Absolutely not!" He believes that you need to have expertise in whatever enterprise you are leading.

The biggest impression I got was how much Walsh loves football. He really doesn't want to do anything other than coach football. All during his talk I was thinking about how much I miss coaching basketball. Hope this coaching job comes through!

It didn't take long. I got a call from the district office telling me I had the Fremont job. The caller seemed a little taken aback when I told her that I was glad to hear it but that I was waiting to hear from School X (and I hadn't even gotten an interview at that point). It wasn't the way things were done—to have the coach get to choose which school he wanted to coach for.

As it turned out I didn't get an offer from School X so I didn't have to make a decision between the two schools, but there was still *the* decision, whether to do this potentially crazy-making thing at all.

The Five-Year Rule

In the spring of 1973, when Sandra and I were students at the Center for Teaching and Learning, at the University of North Dakota, I got a call from Gerald Wolfe, the principal of Yellowstone Elementary School in Rock Springs, Wyoming. Mr. Wolfe invited Sandra and me to Rock Springs to interview for teaching jobs in an energy boom town that was having trouble finding enough qualified teachers for their bulging class-rooms. We were enchanted, with visions of moose and geysers and mountains. As we drove west from Rawlins on I-80 we began to get a different perspective. This was not Yellowstone Park. It was the Red Desert, a land that we later came to love dearly. However, the sagebrush and the empty, wide-open spaces were a shock at the time.

Teachers were indeed in short supply in Rock Springs. Sandra and I traveled to Wyoming with Gary Rasche, a classmate who was also graduating with a teaching degree. Not only did they offer all three of us jobs, but when Arlo Neiderer, the assistant superintendent, found out that Gary's wife, Suzanne—who was pregnant and hadn't accompanied us to Wyoming—was also a teacher, he offered her a job, sight unseen!

When we returned to Grand Forks, we were amazed at how green everything was. Compared to Sweetwater County, Wyoming, eastern North Dakota seemed a garden spot. In spite of our initial reactions, we signed contracts to teach and live in Rock Springs. The bottom line in our minds was that we would always wonder what it would have been like in Wyoming if we had turned away from the challenge of living and teaching in a boom town in the desert. If we didn't like it, we could look for other jobs at the end of the first year. But, if we didn't at least try it, we would always have an itch that couldn't be adequately scratched without a time machine. We ended up loving the place and stayed for three years, leaving only when I was admitted to graduate school at the University of Oregon.

Over time, this process evolved into what I call the Five-Year Rule. Whenever I have a major decision to make I ask myself "How will I feel about this decision (either way) in five years?" Often this will clarify the risks and rewards in ways that haven't been obvious.

In the case of my coaching decision, the question was a no-brainer. In five years, if I don't take the coaching job, I will always wonder what would have happened. If I hate it, or if it is just too stressful given my other responsibilities, I can always gut it out through one year and then quit. Then, when I look back from five years hence, at least I will know that I don't want to do that anymore.

In retrospect, I realize the decision was pretty much locked in when I called my wife right after being offered the job. "Talk me out of this!" I told Sandra. "I think I'm going to do it."

"Talk me out of this!" is a common phrase in my life. I get excited about possibilities and rarely do a cost-benefit analysis before jumping into a new challenge or opportunity. I suspect the phrase may have resonance to many entrepreneurs and leaders. People get excited about things that mean something to them, and that excitement can produce results far beyond what a rational cost-benefit analysis might predict. There is an adage that, if you want something done, get a busy person to do it, partly because there is a momentum to important work that can carry over into other important work. Leaders who approach every new idea with a solely rational decision framework may not find themselves overworked, but they also will miss a lot of excitement.

At this point Sandra easily could have dissuaded me. Fortunately, she didn't even try, or this book might never have happened. "No, do it. You'll have fun. We'll come and watch your games."

Over time I have come to see that the five-year rule contains a subtle "bias for action," to use Tom Peters' and Robert Waterman's famous phrase. A recent essay on regret by Jenijoy La Belle makes this point:

> . . . in the long run, most of us grieve more over non-acts than over acts. A poem by W.S. Merwin starts with: "Something I've not done is following me." It may be these ghostly footsteps and not our missteps that pursue us forever—the wasted possibility, the timid refusal to take a risk, the hesitation when seconds count.
> *San Jose Mercury News*, January 5, 1997)

I still had the thought that maybe I was literally crazed, like those football fans whose wives have to shoot a shotgun through the television set to get their attention during the weeks leading up to the Super Bowl. But, once I had the support of my wife and the permission of my boss, I was committed. I had passed the point of no return. No ghostly footsteps were going to haunt my life. I was a high school basketball coach!

Chapter 1

Hard Beginnings:
The Birth of the Women Warriors

To begin is the hard part.

—Cowboy Bob

In September 1987 I interviewed for the job of director of the Public Management Program at the Stanford Graduate School of Business. To say that I wanted this job was a drastic understatement. I knew that if I got the position my life would never be the same. Right after the interview my family and I went off to Yosemite National Park for a vacation, having been told that a decision would be made by Friday. Friday afternoon found us scrambling down from Nevada Falls, scurrying to get to a phone by five o'clock so I could see if I had the job before everyone went home for Labor Day weekend.

It took us longer than I thought to come down so we didn't get to a phone until after 5:30. I was highly discouraged. Now I would have to wait through the entire long weekend, distracted from the beauty all around me by the uncertainty of whether I would get the job of my dreams. I decided to call anyway and to my surprise, Jim Patell, the

9

Associate Dean in charge of the PMP, was still in the office. He told me that I had the job.

I remember sitting in front of the campfire that night long after Sandra and Gabriel had gone to sleep in the tent. I was captured by the excitement of the adventure I was about to begin and couldn't sleep. Shortly after that the fear began to mix with the excitement. There is a Chinese saying "Be careful what you wish for, you might get it." Now I had what I wanted and I wanted to make the best possible first impression.

First Impressions

I had recently observed the entrance of a new manager to my division at Hewlett Packard. I had been schooled in how a new leader makes an entrance into an organization years before by Fred Miller, who shared with me how he successfully won over the staff of the embattled Oregon Department of Energy. Miller replaced a director, fired by the Governor, who was highly popular with the agency's employees. He came in at a time of crisis and against the wishes of most of its employees. Later I saw in person how Lynn Frank made a quite different, but also highly successful, entrance into the same department after Fred left.

I had heard that this new H-P manager came with good experience at several high-tech companies and there were high hopes among the staff that he would make needed changes. Anticipating (and hoping) that I might soon be making an entrance of my own, I wondered how he was going to go about it.

Big letdown. I was amazed at how little thought he seemed to have given to the first impression he was making. When introduced by the senior VP as the new division head, the new man waved to us and promised to address us soon. A week or so later, at our regularly weekly meeting, his first as our official chief poobah, he had nothing to say, although he did at least speak. After he'd made two appearances before us, I had absolutely no idea of what he was like, where he wanted to take our division, what changes he might want us to undertake, and whether things were going to be different or pretty much the same. The guy left no footprints!

I soon left for Stanford without ever getting an idea what his agenda was. About six months later I ran into a former Hewlett Packard colleague who told me that the division head had already left H-P. I was not surprised, given his lack of message. I believed he had blown an opportunity and I was determined that I would not similarly blow my opportunity to make a good first impression at Stanford by setting some standards and expectations that would help us achieve ambitious goals.

I was up most of the night before the Public Management Program orientation—at which I would first meet the incoming PMP students as the new director—working and reworking and practicing what I would say. Earlier that night, my son (then in fourth grade) had drawn a picture of how he imagined my supervisor at Hewlett Packard had looked when I told him I was leaving to take a job at Stanford. He had just been promoted and was counting on me to replace him, so he was not especially thrilled by my news. Gabriel's drawing captured that emotional state perfectly.

I began my talk by telling the students about the decision to leave a well-paying job that I had worked very hard to get to follow my heart. I related my conversation with my son the night before and put a transparency of Gabriel's drawing on the overhead projector. The room erupted in a sweet roar of laughter at the sight of his gruesome caricature. I went on to give the speech of my life and I became the leader of the PMP in that moment.

I was now determined to make the same kind of splash in my first motivational speech before my new team at Fremont High School.

Journal Entry—May 26, 1994

First team meeting. I was so nervous about meeting the girls for the first time and I had prepared a big motivational talk. What a letdown! Only four of them showed up. I ended up not giving my speech, since it seemed so weird given the situation. The meeting was in a classroom and many of the students didn't leave during lunch. They were more than a little rowdy, so my natural nervousness was compounded by being in an environment over which I had little control.

It turns out that the meeting was announced in the school newsletter, but "no one ever reads that" according to one of the girls. I can't seem to get phone numbers for any of the girls who weren't there. I'm beginning to think that the logistical challenges of simple things are going to be major problems in this job.

It's interesting working in an environment like the Stanford Business School, where so much happens so effortlessly. I'm reminded of Douglass North's lecture on transaction costs back when he was a visiting scholar at the GSB in 1988. North says that the reason some cultures advance and others don't has to do with transaction costs. In the United States we go into a store to buy a pair of shoes. We buy the shoes from a sales clerk we don't know. The shoes were made by people we don't know. We pay for them with a credit card and we don't know any of the people who process the transaction.

Contrast this with a culture in which the shoes are made by someone we know. We talk with them at length about the shoes, we negotiate the price of the shoes (in eggs or vegetables or other barter), we finally agree on a deal. North's point is that if a culture requires people to know each other to do business and the individual transactions take so much time and effort, that culture is not going to grow economically as rapidly as one in which transactions are handled more efficiently.

At the GSB most routine transactions are very efficient. People call you back when you call them. Much business is done by e-mail or voicemail to avoid telephone tag. We are freed up to put most of our intellectual energy into getting the creative part of our jobs done.

I will need to figure out how to deal with the frustration of having routine things take so much time and energy. I asked the four girls to try to get the word out so we could meet next week with everyone. I found out that the JV team, which is in a spring league, was having open gym that afternoon, so I decided I'd go talk to the JV girls in person and tell them about the team meeting next week. Open gym was a revelation. Amalia has some talent, I was glad to find, but the rest seemed a disorganized, out-of-control bunch. Lots of bad attitudes and poor work habits. It will be interesting.

I heard recently that North had won a Nobel prize for his work on institutions. I'm not surprised.

Establishing Credibility

I knew that one of my first and most important tasks was to establish credibility as a coach with my players. I wanted them to believe that they were getting a competent coach, even though I still had some doubts myself.

Fortunately, we had covered this very issue in Learning to Lead a few weeks before. Jerry Porras invited fellow faculty member Charles O'Reilly to speak about research he had done on advertising "source credibility." Professor O'Reilly noted that huge amounts of money ride on the credibility of spokespersons who advertise products on television, radio, and the print media. Picking a credible person to pitch your product is not something that large companies do lightly.

O'Reilly noted three sources of credibility for pitch-persons: expertise, trustworthiness, and something he characterized as "dynamism."

Expertise

Expertise is pretty straightforward. An ideal spokesperson is someone who knows what he is talking about. It wasn't a coincidence that tobacco companies used medical doctors to recommend their cigarettes for their "smoothness" in the 1950s. Robert Young, who played Marcus Welby, MD, so convincingly on television, became an attractive pitchman for medical products after his television series ended. Before-and-after pictures of people who have lost weight, gained muscles, or grown hair over bald spots are useful for the same reason.

I've always loved the loopy "Ask Dr. Science" bits on National Public Radio. Dr. Science is asked some perfectly legitimate question like "What causes lightning?" He goes on a riff that starts out sounding reasonable but ends up being totally and hilariously absurd. The first time I heard him, I was completely taken in for much of his answer. It always ends with a disclaimer: an announcer cautions us that Dr. Science is not a real doctor. "He has a master's degree (pause) *in science*!!!!"

My task was clear. I had to do better than Dr. Science. I needed to demonstrate to my players that I knew enough basketball to be able to provide them with offensive and defensive systems that would give them the best shot at winning games and championships. Beyond that, I wanted to convince them that I knew how to help them unlock their potential to be the best they could be, as basketball players and as people.

Having never coached at the high school level, I was at a bit of a disadvantage. Some people might be impressed that I was an administrator at the Stanford Business School, but it wasn't at all clear to me that this group of girls would think it was any big deal. I decided I would mention my job but not dwell on it. I figured it wouldn't hurt to drop Tara VanDerveer's name since she had recently been a guest lecturer in Learning to Lead and my players were ga-ga over the Stanford women's basketball team. I also planned to stress my role in creating Cupertino Hoops, a co-ed league that had produced many star players for the girls' teams at nearby Monta Vista, Homestead, Lynbrook, and Cupertino High Schools (but not, alas, at Fremont). Also that I had written a book on coaching—although I was pretty ambivalent about that because, as a midwestern Scandanavian type, it seemed unseemly to be so self-promotional. Beyond that, they'd just have to take it on faith that I knew something about coaching high school basketball until I could prove it on the court.

Trustworthiness

Trust is a little more complicated than expertise because the question really is, *what* can I trust you to do?

I remember reading an article about a leader of the Students for a Democratic Society in the 1960s who was a nasty, egotistical bully. When someone asked some SDS members why they supported this fellow, they responded "Because he's *our* nasty, egotistical bully." This leader used his dark talents on their behalf and they trusted him to do the right thing for them. His personal idiosyncrasies were easily forgiven because they believed he had their best interests in mind.

So the issue isn't so much "Is this person honest under every circumstance?" but "Is he going to do right by *me*?"

This seemed to be the way many voters viewed the 1996 Presidential election. Senator Dole tried to make trust and integrity an issue, but with the economy doing well, enough voters felt that President Clinton was going to do right by them even though they may not have trusted him completely in other areas.

My task here was to convince my players that I had their best interests as individuals at heart. I wasn't there just to win basketball games but also to help them develop their potential and have a good experience.

Ever since *Positive Coaching* was published, I have gotten requests to speak to groups of coaches and teachers. Trying to boil down a 400-page book into a 45-minute talk, I began to focus on how coaches motivate. I developed a little framework I call the "Wheel of Internal Motivation," which I use to describe how individuals can become self-motivators to achieve the goals they really want to achieve. I intended to run through this with my players, to communicate to them that I was someone who could help them become the best players they could be and, in the process, forge them into a hugely successful team.

Dynamism

This characteristic is a bit murkier, but it boils down to personal attractiveness. Different pitchpersons are attractive to difference customer groups. Someone like Dennis Rodman, anathema to many "soccer moms" (and dads), may be a perfect pitch man for products aimed at rebellious teenagers. A large part of his appeal to this group may be exactly *because* mom and dad dislike him.

As a second-year MBA student at Stanford, I was determined to get a job with a high-tech company, Hewlett Packard being my first choice. The GSB's Career Management Center (CMC) offered students video-taped "mock interviews" with alumni from the industries in which they were interested. I signed up for an interview with an alum from a local high-tech firm. When the mock interview ended, I was sure I had aced it. I had good answers for every single question and felt I had conveyed a lot of enthusiasm for working in high tech.

When the de-brief with the interviewing alum began I was shocked to discover that he saw me as a "low-energy person." How could he think that? Later, when I viewed the videotape, I understood why. I hesitated before just about every question. Each response took me a few "uhs" and "ahs" before I hit my stride. I radiated listlessness! I begged Uta Kremer of the CMC for another chance. She wasn't supposed to let me have more than one, but she let me have a second mock interview with another alum later that week. (Perhaps the fact that both Uta and I are North Dakota natives caused her to take pity on me!)

For the second interview I cranked up my energy level and was very confident that I had done extremely well. Again, the interviewer commented on my low energy. Again, when I studied the videotape I saw that she was correct. Even though in my head I felt like I was blowing her away with my energy and enthusiasm, in the real world as captured by the camera, I was a bit of a slug.

Now I was really discouraged. I had blown not one but two opportunities and didn't have the nerve to ask Uta for a third try. However, the next week I ran into her in the hall. It turned out that a student had just canceled for a mock interview that afternoon and if I were willing to go home and put on a suit I could have the open slot.

I had learned my lesson. This seemed both like a reprieve and my last chance. My goal was to show so much energy and enthusiasm that during the feedback session, the interviewer would tell me that I needed to tone it down a bit! As luck would have it, this alum worked for Hewlett Packard! I poured so much energy into answering each question that I thought his ears must be ringing by the end of the interview. I almost felt silly acting that way, but with the humiliation of the two previous interviews top-of-mind, I bludgeoned my way through. His first reaction during the debrief was that I had conveyed "a lot of good energy." "Good energy"?? I had virtually shouted my way through the interview and he was telling me I had "good energy"?

Once again I checked myself out on the videotape replay. I discovered that I wasn't loud or obnoxious at all. I came across as confident and enthusiastic in an entirely proper way, just as he had said. In fact, we hit it off so well that he referred me to a GSB classmate of his at H-P who was looking for someone "just like you." A few weeks later I had a job offer from Hewlett Packard!

From this I learned that energy and enthusiasm appear different in the midwestern Scandanavian culture from which I had emerged and the more cosmopolitan and hard-charging culture of a business center like Silicon Valley. I remembered reading some research about loud people, the kind of folks who get right up next to your face and speak **really loud**. It turns out that many loud-ites feel inside their heads as if they are almost whispering. They're seriously out of touch with how much volume they project. It seemed I was the energy projection reverse-equivalent of a loud-ite.

Over the years, I have fine-tuned my internal energy-level sensor, but I was determined to demonstrate how excited I was about this team in my initial meetings with my players. If I erred, it would be on the side of being too exuberant with my new team.

Journal Entry—June 4, 1994

Finally got pretty much the whole team together. This time we met in the coach's office adjacent to the big gym, where there were no distractions. I gave my big motivational speech and for the life of me I couldn't tell how it went over. I'm used to boys, who react (often inappropriately, it's true) when you say something. I don't know if girls are different in general or if this is a particularly quiet group, but if I hoped to have them pumped out of their minds, I'm pretty sure I fell short. They listened politely and showed no disagreement with what I said, but no real enthusiasm either. When I stressed how they could accomplish great things they didn't know they could do if they set goals and worked hard, Lillian threw me for a loop by saying that she wanted to be able to dunk. I didn't respond the way I wish I had. So few women of any size are able to dunk and Lillian is 5 feet 8 at most. I mumbled something like "That's a pretty ambitious goal." What a dorky thing to say! Here I had one person responding to my pep talk and instead of embracing her "stretch" goal, I undoubtedly conveyed skepticism.* What a great motivator I am! Oh, well. At least I don't think I drove anyone off the team.

Having survived, if not exactly distinguished myself, with my entrance as the new coach at Fremont High School, I turned my attention to another issue.

The Name Game

In 1988, Tim Wei became the director of the Stanford Business School's computer facility. This was a challenging assignment for, if there were a predominant word for how most students and faculty felt about the computer facility, it would probably have been *frustrated*. Tim began his tenure as director by changing the name of the organization. "Confucious said that if you do not have the right name, you can never do the right thing," Tim repeated incessantly like a mantra.

---

*Almost exactly one year later, Lillian would win the Central Coast Section triple jump championship!

This was an interesting idea but I was not terribly optimistic about Tim's chances for transforming an organization that seemed immune to any of the prevailing ideas about customer orientation. I was wrong. Tim changed the name to Computer *Services* and the organization quickly became obsessed with meeting its customers' needs. Since I was one of its customers, I was quite pleased with this development. I mention this because, like Tim a few years earlier, I also was a new leader with a name problem.

The Birth of the Women Warriors

For more than forty years, Fremont High School athletic teams had been the "Indians." I had two problems with this. The first was practical.

I was not thrilled with the feminine construction of "Indians." The University of Hawaii mascot is the rainbow. The womens' teams there are the Rainbow Wahini, which I always thought was pretty cool. The Lady Demons are okay. Lady Spartans I have no trouble with, since not many people realize that Helen of Troy was actually from Sparta. But lady Indians were often called squaws, and while I knew that there were many examples of Native American women who engaged in heroic actions on behalf of their people, the name just does not have the kind of connotation I desired. I wanted an image that would help my players visualize what they could become as basketball players and people. *Squaw* just didn't do it.

The second was more philosophic. I thought it was wrong.

I knew that Native Americans had problems being caricatured as mascots, especially by schools that had few, if any, Native American students. Moreover, it struck me as unfriendly to use a symbol of a group of people in a way that is not considered honorable by that group. We live in a time when there are plenty of forces pushing groups away from each other. The high school experience should be a source of developing community rather than fracturing it.

Debra Meyerson taught a Learning to Lead session in which the students were asked to list three things that defined who they were. Doing this exercise myself, I would come up with some combination of husband, father, coach, teacher, or writer depending on the particular day. What is interesting about this exercise is that members of a "majority"

group, such as whites, rarely list race as one of their defining characteristics. Our lists tended to reflect each of us as individuals.

However, people of color almost always mentioned their race as a
defining characteristic. The class discussions after this exercise were invariably intense and compelling. White students would often ask why
race had to be such an important thing to people of color when they, the
white students, didn't get so hung up on it.

One answer is that members of a majority group have privileges that
they take for granted. They tend to assume that they have the right to be
treated as individuals because they pretty much always have been
treated that way. But people of color have experienced their race as a
defining characteristic virtually every day of their life. Once, on a long
plane ride, my wife sat next to a woman of color, a colleague she had
known for many years. This woman had never once mentioned that she
had been the target of discrimination. During the course of this trip,
however, a barrier came down and she shared with Sandra numerous stories about treatment she and her family had received that would set any
feeling person's blood to boil. This was a woman who was extraordinar-
ily successful in the professional world she inhabited, but her achieve-
ments had not exempted her or her family from regular, humiliating
reminders of her minority status.

Many of my players were quite attached to the Indian as the repre-
sentation of their school. I respected my players' affection for the tradi-
tion, but I tended to side with Native Americans who found the use of
Indian as a mascot—complete with headdress—offensive. I began searching for an image that would finesse the school's mascot controversy.

An answer came from several directions at once. Joseph Campbell,
Robert Bly, Gary Snyder and others have written about the power of archetypes in our daily lives. *Archetypes* are models or images embedded
deep in our collective experience and psyches that are often tapped by
poets, artists, and other creative individuals to enrich life. Among the
common archetypes are the trickster, the warrior, and the king. I also
had been taken by the examples of incredible courage and perseverance
shown by women in Maxine Hong Kingston's book *The Woman Warrior*,
especially since there were several Asian-American players (including
one Japanese girl) on my team. Then I read an article in the *Mercury-
News West Magazine* about a woman basketball player. The story, also en-
titled "The Woman Warrior" (July 31, 1994), told of a woman who

regularly played against and held her own with male players. When I shared the article with my players, Shauna suggested we get sweatshirts with "Woman Warriors" on them.

I began to consider the *warrior* archetype as one that could help my players develop attributes of strength and courage by tapping into the "warrior within." As a team we began talking about what it means to be a woman warrior. We used phrases like "fierce and friendly," which I learned from my friend and coaching guru, Jeff McKay. While the game is going on, we play with as much intensity as we can and are not afraid of going hard to the basket, even if it means knocking an opponent down. Once the whistle blows, *then* we help the opponent up. We refuse to demonize the opponent in a pathetic attempt to increase our motivation to win.

I constantly looked for ways to use the warrior image to reinforce habits and personal characteristics that I felt were critical to our being successful. For example, I suggested that warriors work on their "weak side first." Most people like the feeling that comes with success and thus tend to work on the things that they are already good at, while avoiding the discomfort that comes from working on weaknesses. An attribute of a warrior is to recognize weaknesses and work first on gaining strength where she is weak. Since we all like the sensation of success, we tend to find the time to improve areas where we are already strong. This led us always to start our lay-up drills shooting with the left hand (since everyone on the team was righthanded). If we ran out of time, the weak side, which it was critical to improve, would not be shortchanged.

The wonderful thing about *warrior* is that it is neither synonymous with nor excludes Native American culture. The warrior archetype is embedded deep in *human* consciousness. Images of fierce warriors can be found in virtually all societies in every nook and cranny of the world.

I asked my wife if she had any ideas for an image that might have a Native American flavor to it—one that all the players could rally around without arousing negative feelings. A few hours later she came back with an image of a strong and beautiful woman with a basketball rolling off the end of her fingertips. The woman warrior motif served to reinforce in our team the goal of becoming strong athletes (and ultimately successful individuals) and we began to refer to our team as the Women Warriors of Fremont. My wife designed a logo using her image and at the end of summer league I gave T-shirts with WWF to each player with this image on it.

There is one more, painful aspect of beginning a new leadership position that needs addressing.

Fear and Courage on the Basketball Court

David Hilfiker, in his remarkable book about the medical profession *Healing the Wounds*, talks about the undiscussable reality that every doctor faces: killing a patient. He notes that it is unavoidable—sooner or later every doctor will make a mistake that will result in the completely avoidable death of someone. Given that this happens to virtually every doctor, what is remarkable, according to Hilfiker, is that doctors almost never talk about this or the guilt that results.

I don't mean to compare coaching as a profession with medicine, although at their best both result in improved human beings. But we coaches have an undiscussable of our own. We don't talk about our anxiety over how well our teams (and thus we, as coaches) will do. "Anxiety" is really a euphemism. *Fear* is the grittier but more accurate term.

Coaches don't like to talk about fears partly because coaching tends to be such a macho profession. To admit fears about one's competency to another coach might—likely would—be interpreted as weakness. Athletics is often compared to the military, which may also have a taboo about verbalizing fears of going into battle.

However, effective military leaders have learned to face their fear and manage it rather than deny its existence. Larry Donnithorne, in *The West Point Way of Leadership* notes "Fear is not a bad teacher. Fear strips one of pretensions and flattens false bravado. Fear brings a person face to face with the best and the worst of who he really is."

Part of the taboo on voicing one's fears stems from confusing fearlessness with courage. *Fearlessness* is exactly what it says—a lack of fear. *Courage* is more complicated. Courage not only implies the presence of fear, it includes acknowledging and facing it.

Having been raised on the plains of North Dakota, I am afraid of the ocean. And my experience body surfing in Baja didn't help. A wave picked me up and deposited me gracelessly and painfully head first into the sand. In a confused panic, I picked myself up and began to stumble out to sea! Fortunately my son, Gabriel, was watching out for me. He came rushing in to lead me to safety on shore. For me, surfing would be a courageous, if foolhardy, act. On the other hand, Gabriel, who grew up in California, loves being in the ocean, spending every free hour surfing. He isn't demonstrating courage because he isn't afraid. If you do something that you are not afraid of, you are not showing courage, even if the feat in question is something that other people fear. However, the first time Gabriel went surfing, with a rented board clearly labeling him as a flat-lander wannabee beach boy—now that took courage!

After the elation of getting the Fremont coaching job subsided, I became aware of my fears: of failure, of looking foolish, of making a bad decision in the crucial waning moments of a game, of lacking time to learn enough to become a good coach, among others.

I realized the normal fears that accompany any new challenge were intensified because I had written *Positive Coaching*. I imagined people who had read *Positive Coaching* coming to see my team play and going away thinking the book was written by a fraud!

I have learned over the years that fear leads so easily to procrastination. When I am afraid, I tend to put off dealing with the source of the fear, particularly when the day of reckoning is far off in the future. "It is still several months until the start of the season," I tell myself. "I don't need to worry today about what I will do the first week of practice. I can enjoy life today and still have plenty of time to deal with it."

By writing about my fears and sharing them with Sandra and friends like Jeff McKay, I found they seemed less scary. In Colonel Donnithorne's words, "Unless you face your fear, it will be a constant and limiting partner." I also knew that as some very wise person had once said, "The greater part of courage is in having done the thing before." I just needed to get through the stress of the hard beginnings and I would be fine.

Take-Aways

Getting Started

1. Recognize that you have only one chance to make a first impression.
   a. Think through what you want to convey in that first encounter because you may never again have such an attentive audience. Your players (and in some cases their parents) are eager to understand where you are coming from.
   b. Focus on the most important things (no more than three for maximum impact), and figure out how to emphasize them throughout your first session with your players.
   c. Practice your remarks for your first meeting(s) with your team so that by the time you speak to them you feel comfortable with your message and delivery.
   d. Be careful not to put too much pressure on yourself. You don't have to be perfect in making your first impression.

2. Develop a plan to establish your credibility with your new team. Think about how you can present your experience and credentials in a way that will relate to them, in particular:
   a. How your expertise will help them accomplish their goals.
   b. That you understand their needs and can be trusted to not betray them.
   c. That you are excited about coaching them and that you demonstrate to them that you have the necessary dynamism to make them successful.

3. Look for ways to establish a special identity with an organizational name or nickname. If none exists, come up with one of your own that fits with the unique characteristics of what you are trying to accomplish with this team.
   a. Look for a tangible symbol of this identity that you can give to each player—a t-shirt or other totem that will provide a constant reminder of what this team is all about.

4. Look at your own anxieties and fears about coaching. Talk about them with close friends whom you can trust to give you support and encouragement.

5. Remember that Cowboy Bob was right. The hardest part is often the beginning. You'll get through it and things will get better. Hang in there!

Chapter 2

High Hopes and Harsh Reality: Goals That Change Behavior

A demanding performance challenge tends to create a team. The hunger for performance is far more important to team success than team-building exercises, special incentives, or team leaders with ideal profiles. In fact, teams often form around such challenges without any help or support from management. Conversely, potential teams without such challenges usually fail to become teams.

—Jon Katzenbach and Douglas Smith
The Wisdom of Teams

Here is some conventional wisdom about effective goal setting: Set goals that are achievable but challenging; write down your goals—goals that aren't written are rarely achieved; make sure your goals are measurable; and monitor your progress regularly.

Conventional wisdom is fine but I wanted to go beyond it and use the goal-setting process to *power* the team. Gene Webb, a mentor of mine at the GSB before his untimely death, often said that you can smell emotional commitment a mile away. I wanted my players reeking of emotional commitment, and I believed that a big part of what made a team reek was goals that motivated.

Fortunately, we had just explored the role that goals play in Learning to Lead. Garry Wills had recently come out with his book *Certain Trumpets*. In an excerpt in *The Atlantic* magazine, he discusses the central role that goals play in the dynamic between leaders and followers.

The Link Between Leaders and Followers

Wills described how his father became his leader when he was a young man, even though he intended to rebel against him. His father figured out his son's goals and devised means to get young Garry to do his bidding, because in so doing he would further his own goals.

Wills points out the absurdity of the belief in the "great man" theory of leadership (in which the unwashed masses are bent to the will of the leader because of his superior will or ability): "So far I have been discussing just two things—leaders and followers. That is better, at least, than discussions dealing with only one thing—leaders. But the discussions cannot get far without the goal. This is not something added on to the other two. It is the reason for the existence of the other two. It is also the equalizer between leader and followers. The followers do not submit to the person of the leader. They join him or her in pursuit of the goal."

That explained a lot to me about why people sometimes stay in abusive relationships. A battered woman who believes she has no other realistic means of supporting herself and her children may feel she has no choice but to return to her husband to obtain food, shelter, and clothing for her children. She can always hope that he will change his abusive behavior, which may seem more likely to her than that she will be able to get a job paying enough to support her kids. The primacy of her goal of taking care of her kids links her to a tyrannical family leader.

Similarly, an athlete who wants more than anything to make it to the Olympics may willingly subject herself or himself to an authoritarian coach who has trained previous Olympic champions. As long as athletes believe the coach can deliver the goods, they may be willing to put up with highly demeaning treatment.

The incredible power that shared goals can bring means that getting a team to commit to achieving ambitious goals is one of the most critical tasks of a coach. But there is a problem with goals.

The Randomness of Goals

Years ago when I was an MBA student, an advertising executive came to talk about the wildly successful Levi's 501 campaign that made *the* hottest fashion item out of a pair of jeans that had been around since the 1800s. He talked about the fickleness of the fashion business. When pressed by one of the students to give up his secrets, he said that with fashion you "throw a bunch of things up against the wall and some of them stick. You're never quite sure which ones are going to stick and, after they do, you're never quite sure why they did."

I have often thought that this was a good description of how goals work for most people. Many of us have been inspired more than once as the new year arrives to set goals that, if achieved, would have improved our lives. But there seems to be a randomness about which goals we are able to work toward and which are quickly forgotten. Some stick to the wall, most don't.

For coaches this is a sobering thought, because the literature on teams is pretty clear that outstanding performance is driven by the establishment of challenging goals. I doubt that there are very many coaches around the world who don't set goals for their teams at the beginning of each year. I also venture to say that most of those goals don't—in the immortal words of Humphrey Bogart—amount to a hill of beans.

So let me put into my own words a lesson I have learned about goals and goal-setting:

Goals should change people's behavior.

If our goals don't cause us to work harder, or longer, or smarter, or to spend our time differently, or to acquire new skills or all of these, then they are useless. Simply *setting* goals doesn't do anything. There is a line familiar to anyone who has ever been in a twelve-step program: The program only works if you work the program. But all too often, we don't work the program, and the goals we set don't motivate us to change our behavior.

Journal Entry—November 2, 1994

I gave a fire-and-brimstone speech yesterday in practice. Uncharacteristic for me. The day before was Halloween and only about 10 girls showed up for practice—varsity and JV combined. All the varsity players who aren't still out for volleyball or field hockey were there, but large numbers of the JV players were AWOL. It turns out that they had complained among themselves about having to go to practice on Halloween and some bright mind (I wonder who!) ventured that the coaches couldn't punish them all if they took the day off to get an early start on trick-or-treating.

After practice, Jason and Lori were emphatic that the no-shows needed to be punished and were itching to do something that would send a message. I agreed that we needed to establish a standard. You don't get high performance standards without having discipline, and enforcing discipline is an important leadership task. I prefer, as I'm sure everyone does, to have people impose discipline on themselves, but that wasn't one of the options in this instance. Since Jason is the JV coach, we agreed that after practice he would take the no-shows (all JV players) out to the track for an additional workout while the others would be rewarded by being sent home at the regular time.

On the way home I realized that I needed to be the one to deliver this message, even though either Lori and Jason would gladly have done it. First, I want to establish myself as the leader of the entire program, not just of the varsity. There is so much symbolism attached to the messenger in situations like this. A second reason is that I wanted a surgical strike—one that would cut quickly without lots of bad feelings lingering. I was afraid that my assistants, having come up through systems more authoritarian than I want to establish here, might overdo the punishment angle. The third reason is that I don't like doing this sort of thing and I need to get more comfortable with it. I like being the "white hat" guy and don't like to confront people about their failure to perform. Here was a chance to push out from my comfort zone. Finally, I think that the message in situations like this is so easily misinterpreted by those being punished. I wanted to make sure for myself that it was clearly communicated *why* the consequence was being imposed, that it was not punishment for punishment's sake.

On the way to practice yesterday I thought about the ideas I wanted to communicate. I just got our letter about the Mt. Pleasant tournament that mentioned that Presentation wouldn't be in the tournament this year after having won it for each of the last four or five years. The Mt. Pleasant coach wrote that the rest of us now had a chance to win the tournament for a change. I decided to use that as the center of my message. I actually got way into the theatrics of it, booming and lowering my voice, ranting and raving. Referring to the Mt. Pleasant letter, I said that our goal as a program was not to be better than Cupertino or Saratoga or the other teams in our league. Our goal was to be the kind of program about which other coaches and teams are saying "I'm glad Fremont isn't in this tournament any more so we have a chance to win it." I asked them if they thought the girls trying to make the Presentation team skipped practice on Halloween, and answered myself with "I don't THINK so!" I was happy with my oratorical performance and practice today was one of our best so far.

Goals Going Nowhere

I had my share of experiences, positive and negative, with goal setting for the Women Warriors. Let's start with some of the mistakes, the goals that went nowhere, the ones that didn't stick to the wall, even though some of them may actually have been good ideas.

The Forest and the Trees

One big mistake I made in my first year (1994–95) was having way, way too many goals. As a team, we set goals per game for the number of free throws we wanted to shoot, for rebounds, for turnovers (which had its own problem—see next section), for how many 30-second clock violations we wanted to force the other team into, for how many points we wanted to score and how few we wanted to allow the other team, and on and on. We had so many goals that it became impossible for us to concentrate on all (or perhaps on any) of them. Twenty free throws a game is a useful goal but, because it was buried in a forest of goals, its utility as a lone tree pointing the way to our destination got lost. Consequently we lost some needed focus and intensity.

The other problem with this approach was that it was pretty mechanical and detached from what the purpose of having goals was all about. Each individual goal may have made sense, but in total they didn't. What I really wanted wasn't twenty free throws—that was just a surrogate for having an aggressiveness on offense that rocked the defense back on its heels. If we got less than twenty free throw attempts, it probably meant that we weren't being aggressive enough in taking the ball to the basket.

Too many goals made it easy for me to lose sight of the bigger picture. I failed to relentlessly remind the team of the purpose behind the goals—something that might have made a difference in several close games that year. The second problem with my goal setting arose because I forgot a principle I had learned many years before.

The Dog That Didn't Bark

There is a famous Arthur Conan Doyle story in which Sherlock Holmes solves the mystery at hand by realizing that the most important clue is something that *didn't* happen. While others focused only on what happened, he noted that the dog that had always barked before *didn't* bark on the night in question. Understanding why the dog didn't bark was the key to cracking the case. It was the genius of that story to take advantage of the reader's natural tendency to focus more on happenings that can be observed than a happening that happens to be a non-happening! There is wisdom in Doyle's story for coaches regarding goal-setting.

In my first year of coaching I set a goal for the team to not have more than eight turnovers per game. This violated a principle I had learned more than twenty years earlier working with emotionally disturbed children at the Behavioral Learning Center in St. Paul, Minnesota: Kids (of all ages) do better with goals that are framed to increase a positive behavior rather than to eliminate or reduce an inappropriate behavior.

Although the staff was encouraged by Shirley Pearl, the school's principal, and Don Challman, the social worker, to set positive behavioral goals for our little rascals, invariably we were tempted toward goals that consisted of *not* doing what drove us crazy (**Greg**: *I will not tease Judy and cause her to get upset*; **Judy**: *I will not punch Greg when he teases me*. **Randy**: *I will not take anything that doesn't belong to me*; **Kevin**: *I will not swear at Mr. Thompson when I don't get my way*.)

Over time we learned, often the hard way, that our students did much better if they were trying to *do* something rather than *refrain* from doing something.

Fast-forwarding back to 1994–95, my players were so focused on *not* making a turnover that we played timidly and often made really silly turnovers on passes that weren't going anywhere even had they been completed. Finally I came to my senses and told the players where I had gone wrong. I suggested that we no longer focus on reducing turnovers but rather on *making good passes* that would lead to baskets. After practice, Shelly came to me sighing in relief. She had felt terribly constricted in her play as point guard by having a negative goal of not making a mistake, in effect trying to keep the dog from barking.

William Glasser asserts in *Positive Addiction* that it is easier to replace a negative habit with a positive one than it is to simply stop the negative habit. Sandra and I heard Dr. Glasser speak at a workshop in Logan, Utah, in 1975, the summer before his book came out. Later that summer Sandra gave up smoking with relative ease by replacing her addiction to smoking with the positive actions of daily yoga exercises.

Why did I set a no-barking goal when I knew all this? I think we often act in ways that are inconsistent with the lessons of our own experience, as I did here. The world is a complicated place and many people have a lot of things going on in their lives. I guess we just can't be like Sherlock every time.

My other goal-setting mistake was actually a good idea that I failed to implement properly.

Shooting Clubs

I am convinced that "natural" shooting touches can be acquired during the off-season through practice—lots and lots of practice. (As one basketball camp flier I received says, "Great teams are made during the season. Great players are made in the off-season.") I had seen my son become an outstanding shooter several years earlier by taking 500 to 1,000 shots every day over a period of several months.

During the off-season between my first and second year of coaching, I came up with the idea of awarding T-shirts to players when they had taken 10,000 shots, 25,000 shots, 50,000 shots, etc. When a player finished taking her 10,000 shots—recorded on a daily workout sheet—she would get a T-shirt with a cool graphic design (perhaps a player atop a mountain of basketballs) with a caption something like "Member of the 10,000 Shot Club."

When I mentioned this to my players, they seemed excited. However, when I asked them periodically how they were doing with their shooting, I found that most of them weren't shooting much on their own, and those who were weren't bothering to record it. At one point I took a couple of the team leaders aside and told them that I'd really like to be able to give them the 10,000 Shot Club T-shirt to motivate the rest of the team to do more shooting. Would they please start taking and recording their shots so the rest of the team would get motivated? They nodded their assent, but nothing came of it.

I still think this is a terrific idea but it didn't work in this instance for a couple of reasons. For one thing, it was too abstract. I failed to make it tangible enough. If I had gotten a really cool T-shirt designed and had one in hand to show the players, it might have made a big difference. The *idea* of the T-shirt in the absence of the *actual* T-shirt, wasn't enough to motivate a change in behavior.

Whenever I am asked for my short list of the most important characteristics or behaviors of effective leadership, I always include follow-up. There are more good ideas in the world than you can shake a stick at. None of them are worth anything unless someone puts energy behind them. In this case, I simply didn't put sufficient energy behind this pretty good (perhaps even outstanding) idea. I didn't pay attention to my own short list!

I also needed to focus more on getting "early adopters," the first one or two players to actually do this. There is always some inertia in something that requires self-discipline and sacrifice. Once someone got the T-shirt in a ceremony in front of the rest of the team and then got to wear it at work-outs, I believe that others would have been motivated to do their shooting so they also could get one. I could have scheduled workout sessions with a couple of the players to help them through the hard parts in the beginning and get them comfortable both with the shooting and the charting. I did suggest that they keep track of the number of shots they took in a 10-minute period. Then they could shoot without having to count every shot. Had I worked with them to help them get that 10-minute count, the idea might have taken root.

But the kicker here is that those things would have required a lot of my time and energy during a time of the year when I was trying to recover from burnout from the season that had just ended. And, as I think about it, perhaps the players themselves were feeling some burnout. It is hard to be intense about basketball all year round. They probably were feeling a need to get away from it as well. And, maybe I just didn't want it badly enough.

Goals That Stuck to the Wall

I've already alluded to the fact that goal setting is more an art than a science. When goals have an intuitive "just-right" feel for an individual or team, they can work a kind of magic. Like anything else, there is a learning curve in goal-setting. Not having coached a high school team before, I simply didn't know enough about setting appropriate goals. But that's okay. Our goal-setting as a team improved a lot in year two. Let me describe some goals that helped us develop as a team.

Better Every Week

I was struck by the goal that Bill Walsh set for the San Francisco 49ers when he became head coach: Play better every week. He believed that they didn't yet have the talent to win very many games, so a goal of winning every week would have served as a big discourager. But continuous improvement is something that any individual or team can embrace. In my second year of coaching we set the goal of playing better this week than last. And, for the most part, we did. This goal helped us deal with the disappointment of getting badly trounced early in the season by more talented teams.

The Best at the End

Perhaps our most behavior-changing goal was to be playing our best basketball at the end. There were two parts to this. The first aspect was that we wanted to be in such good physical condition and have such robust mental toughness that in *each game* we would outplay the other team in the fourth quarter (unless we were way ahead and the game was out of reach). I discuss this in detail in Chapter 5, so I will only mention here that this goal helped keep our focus and motivation regardless of what had happened in the previous three quarters. Like the Continental Basketball Association rules that award points for winning each quarter, this gave us motivation to continue to strive *through* the end of the game. We knew we could always salvage something out of a blow-out loss if we ended strong. In effect, our fourth quarters in losing games were tune-ups for our next game. It also helped us keep our focus in our conditioning drills throughout the season. Players knew each time they ran the dreaded liners that they would receive the benefit in the fourth quarter of the upcoming game. And in virtually every game, they were able to play their hearts out in the last eight minutes.

The second part of this goal was to be playing our best basketball at the end of the year, and both seasons we were a significantly better team at the end than at any other time during the year (see Chapter 6). As is often the case with motivating goals, accomplishing this was directly under the control of the players. They couldn't determine whether they would win or not—that depended a great deal on what the other team did—but if they worked hard physically and learned as much as they could mentally, they absolutely could determine whether they would be playing better ball at the end of the season. In both years I was proud to receive compliments from other coaches who were amazed at how much better our team was at the end of the season than the beginning.

One issue around goal setting was how high to set our sights.

High Hopes

During the off-season after my first season, I had three starters coming back and several other pretty good ballplayers. I vacillated about whether, as a team, we should think about setting the goal of getting to the Central Coast Section championship game, which virtually guaranteed a berth in the NorCal tournament. Setting the goal of winning our league was a no-brainer, since we all believed we could do that. (As it turned out . . . well, you'll have to read on to find out what happened.)

On the one hand I truly believed that, in general, higher goals lead to greater efforts and thus better performance. However I felt insecure about suggesting the CCS finals as a goal. In retrospect, I believe I was afraid of being laughed at. I also worried that my affection and respect for my players might have led me to have unrealistic ideas about how much they could accomplish. Most coaches have had experiences with parents who, against all the evidence, are convinced that their child is the next coming of Sheryl Swoopes or Jennifer Azzi. Perhaps, I worried, I had no sense of reality about my players. And, I was concerned that if we fell far short of that goal it would be hard to deal with the discrepancy between that and what we actually accomplished.

This raises another factor to be considered in setting goals. In negotiations theory there is something called the "range of reasonableness" for offers and counter offers. For example, say someone is selling a car for $20,000. If I offer $5,000, they may just laugh at me. Five thousand dollars may be so far below what they are willing to accept, and below the actual value of the car, that I will hurt my negotiating position with a ridiculous offer that is way out of the range of reasonableness.

On the other hand, if I can determine the approximate range of reasonableness—say $17,000 is the "walk-away price" (the price below which the seller would keep the car rather than sell it), the lower the offer I can make *while still landing in the range of reasonableness*, the better I will do. Whereas an offer of $5,000 just makes me look clueless about the value of automobiles, an offer of $14,000 is within spitting distance of his walk-away price. He may be stimulated to come back with a counter offer below his initial asking price, which can mean savings for me.

My concern was to not approach the players with a goal that was so far outside their range of reasonableness that they wouldn't take it seriously or work hard to achieve it. And, as I stated earlier in this chapter, goals that don't change behavior aren't worth setting.

While I was fretting about this issue, I read something in Dick DeVenzio's book *Stuff! good players should know* that encouraged me to throw caution to the winds. Here's what he has to say about high hopes:

> Don't listen to people who try to keep you from getting your
> hopes up. Get them way up. You can take disappointment later if
> things don't work out. (By then you'll have new hopes and plans
> to think about.) But for right now, aim for the stars. Go for it.

That convinced me to suggest to the players that we shoot not just for our own league title but to make it to the CCS title game, with its accompanying berth in the NorCal tournament. At our awards banquet after the season ended, I told the players and parents that I had been uneasy about our setting such high goals but that, if we failed to reach them, as a team we can help each other adjust to not reaching them. And, in the meantime, having big, exciting goals (what Jim Collins and Jerry Porras in their book *Built to Last* call "big, hairy, audacious goals"), would motivate people to work harder getting ready for the next season.

The Silver Lining in Lop-Sided Games

Over the years I have been in many lop-sided games, more often than I like to admit on the losing side. But even when I am coaching a team that is on the winning end of a lop-sided score, I rarely enjoy it. It just isn't much fun to beat up on a weaker team.

However, there is an upside to lop-sided games. They allow you to work on two kinds of goals that normally don't receive enough attention: "stretch goals" in winning games and "character goals" in losing efforts.

Stretch Goals

Stretch goals are pretty much like they sound. They are goals that appear to be just beyond the reach of the player. If you don't stretch to reach them, or, in some cases, grow and stretch, you won't achieve them. Stretch goals involve some risk, so many coaches tend not to encourage players to go after them because they can result in lower performance in the short run. The payoff is down the road, however, when what used to be a stretch becomes part of a player's normal repertoire. Blow-out games in which your team jumps way out ahead early provide an opportunity for the players to work on stretch goals.

Last year, Phil Kelly, my athletic director, mentioned to me after a game that Chi needed to learn to dribble with her left hand. As soon as he said that I realized that she didn't feel confident dribbling with her left hand. She usually gave up her dribble before I wanted her to whenever she was overplayed to her weak hand. I told Chi what Phil had said and encouraged her to try to penetrate to the basket off a lefthanded dribble at least three times in the next game (which happened to be against a weak team). I encouraged her not to worry about succeeding in her move off her left hand, but to get the three tries in regardless of how the first one goes.

This story had a happy result. Chi used the next game to work on her left hand and made some brilliant lefty moves to the basket; she went on to develop much greater confidence in her left hand during the remainder of the season.

Stretch goals have the ability to transform blow-out victories into teachable moments. When a team gets far ahead of an opponent, there is a seductive tendency to lose focus, to settle back and "enjoy" the rout. Players and teams with stretch goals, however, see a blow-out as a chance to improve a weakness or to develop a tentative skill into a habit.

Character Goals

There is a lot of loose talk about how sports build character. I think of character as something that doesn't usually come into play until there is adversity. It's easy to be honest when you have more money than you need. It's easy to be determined when everything is going your way. It's easy to be gracious when you are winning.

Character kicks in (for better or worse) when you *don't* have enough money. Do you fudge just a bit on your income taxes? When it's windy and rainy and cold, do you still get up out of bed and hit the street to get your run in before work? When the other team is kicking the stuffing out of yours, are you still charitable to the opposing coach?

I once heard a remarkable story about Booker T. Washington. A reporter told him that another "Negro" leader of the time had said some critical things about him. After relating the comments in gory detail, the reporter wondered what Mr. Washington thought about the other fellow. Washington said that he had the highest regard for him, that he had done a lot of good things for other Negroes, and that he was a very smart and honorable man. The reporter couldn't believe his ears. "How can you say that. Didn't you hear what he said about you?" Washington retorted, "Yes, I did, young man, but you asked me what I thought about him, not what he thought about me." That is character!

For a coach concerned about helping players develop character, being on the wrong end of a lop-sided game offers a great opportunity to work on "character goals." Character goals revolve around developing positive character traits such as persistence in the face of adversity, grace under pressure, and treating your opponents with respect. Often the best time to work on a character goal is when performance goals (e.g., winning the game) are beyond reach (i.e., when we are getting the stuffing knocked out of us).

Our most important character goal as a team was to always continue trying as hard as we could regardless of how far we were behind.

Journal Entry—January 10, 1996

Last night we pulled off the most amazing comeback. Against Wilcox, a team that we should be able to beat quite handily, we got way behind in the first half, 35–19. I was so disheartened I had to work really hard at half time to convey the message that we still had a chance to win if we didn't give up. But I did and we didn't. And a miracle happened. We came out in the second half and played like world-beaters. We outscored them 23–4 in the third quarter, and ended up beating them 55–44. Isn't basketball wonderful?!

The Coach's Own Goals

I'm a firm believer in the adage that people are more affected by our example than our rhetoric. Talk is cheap. Action has a price. The coach who sets a clear and positive example of setting and committing to his own goals will have more credibility when he tries to get his players to embrace goal setting.

In this spirit, I shared my own real-time goal-setting experience with my players. I had set a goal at the beginning of 1994 to run an average of two miles per day for the entire year (a total of 730 miles). When I hit that milestone in early September, I decided to try for 1,000 miles for the year. In late December 1994, just before we took a few days off for New Year's, I told my players that they were not the only ones who were setting goals, that I had set a goal of 1,000 miles for the year and I needed 26 miles in the next three days to reach my goal. Knowing that making a public commitment would help motivate me, I encouraged them to ask me about it at our next practice to see if I had made it.

Sure enough the first thing that came up at our first practice in 1995 was whether I had made my 1,000 miles. I did it, but it certainly wasn't easy. I had promised my mother that we would spend the day together on New Year's Eve doing a movie marathon. Since I needed eight miles more to reach 1,000, I hit the streets for a couple of miles in the morning before we went off to see *Little Women*. After going to a restaurant for lunch we went to another theater to see *Pulp Fiction*. (We both liked *Little Women* more than *Pulp Fiction*.) When we got home it was time for dinner. So I didn't get back out on the streets until after 9 o'clock on New

Year's Eve to run my last six miles so I could make my goal (and not incidently so I wouldn't have to tell my players that I hadn't made it!).

I went into gruesome detail about how painful and uncomfortable it had been to go out on New Year's Eve. I wanted them to get the idea that they shouldn't give up on something just because it is difficult or uncomfortable. I also described the elation I felt, like floating on air, as I ran the last couple miles back home knowing that I was going to make my goal. They listened raptly and then we got focused on getting ready for the conference season.

Unmet Goals and the Last Five Minutes

A final note about unmet goals. Goals don't have to be met to be helpful. Although we didn't achieve our goal of making it to the CCS finals in 1996 (it didn't help that the school added enough students between 1995 and 1996 to land us in the tougher Division Two seedings), I believe that setting the goal helped us in a number of ways. It helped create a sense of excitement about the coming year. It got many of the players out for regular early-morning workouts during the summer. It helped them keep basketball as a priority when they had many other competing activities that otherwise might have reduced their commitment. And, for all I know, it might have been essential to our ultimate success. The previous year we had set a goal of winning our league and had come in third. This year we set a much higher goal and that may have given us just that extra little bit of effort that we needed.

George Leonard quotes an old martial arts saying in his book *Mastery*: "The Master is the one who stays on the mat five minutes longer every day than anybody else." Maybe our setting the CCS finals as a goal kept us out on the court each day for those extra five minutes and perhaps that is what ultimately made it possible for us to persevere through our Dark December and ultimately enjoy The Streak. In any event, I don't automatically classify unmet goals as failures as long as they move a person or team forward, as long as they change behavior!

Take-Aways

Goal Setting

1. Remember that the goal of a goal is to change a person's behavior. If the goal doesn't result in the person (or team) working harder, practicing longer, being more willing to experience discomfort, or something, it isn't worth the paper it's written on. Don't set goals just to be setting goals. Make sure you understand what behavioral change you are after.

2. Understand that goal setting is more art than science. Be willing to experiment with goals. Keep the ones that "stick to the wall" and be willing to change the ones that go nowhere.

3. Encourage players to set positive goals—ones that involve increasing a desirable behavior rather than negative goals that try to reduce or eliminate an undesirable behavior.

4. Avoid setting too many goals. Three goals are much easier to focus on than ten.

5. Make sure your players understand the purpose behind the goal. If you set a goal of shooting twenty or more free-throws each game, make sure you remind them from time to time that the purpose of the goal is to encourage them to be aggressive in taking the ball to the basket.

6. Remember that goals often need to develop some momentum. You may have to make a goal tangible to the players by putting some energy into it, stoking the fire at the beginning. If a goal is worth setting, it is worth your following through to do what you can to give it a fighting chance of success.

7. Encourage your players to set both "stretch goals" that they can work on against easier competition and "character goals" to work on when they start to feel overwhelmed by the competition.

8. Don't be afraid to set ambitious goals. As a group you can deal with it if you don't achieve your high hopes. And giving voice to your high hopes can often lead you to achieve more than you would have with so-called realistic goals.

9. Set goals for yourself and share your process and results with your players. This will provide a model for them and may give you some additional impetus to achieve your goals, since players will ask you how you are doing with them!

Abrupt Ending #1

Fremont Frustratingly Close

The most difficult part of losing Saturday, said Fremont girls basketball Coach Jim Thompson, wasn't the loss itself, but that
Fremont was just hitting its peak. The Indians lost seven of their
first eight games, but over the final month of the season, they
won eight of their final eleven. A team that looked like one of the
worst in the Central Coast Section developed into one on the
verge of advancing to the Division III semifinals before it lost to
Sacred Heart Cathedral 65–60 in the quarterfinals. Fremont ral-
lied from a twenty-point deficit to close to within one with 25 seconds left against the Irish. That's when Jenny White, who scored
nine of her game-high 27 points in the fourth quarter, was fouled
and made the first free throw to make the score 61–60. She made
the second, but the point was disallowed because of a lane violation. SHC built on its lead from there. Fremont finished 12–14.

San Jose *Mercury News*
February 28, 1995

E-Mail Message, March 3, 1995

To: Learning to Lead Students
From: Jim Thompson
So, abruptly it ends. I remember thinking I was crazy to take on this
added responsibility last April when I talked with you in class. But

what caused me to try it was the realization that if I didn't, five years later I would regret it. On the other hand, if it turned out to be too much I could always make it through one year and then quit, comforted by the thought that I had at least given it a shot.

So now almost a year later, I find I made the right decision. I will coach Fremont again next year (beyond that, who knows—one year at a time) and already have lots of ideas about how to get past that quarterfinals mark and into the semis and finals.

The take-away I'd like to leave you with is to be open to the opportunity to be a volunteer coach at some point in your life. There is nothing quite like having an impact on young people. One anecdote from this year: About a month ago, after a Thursday night practice, I caught the last few minutes of the Lynbrook-Mountain View game. Lynbrook was the second-place team and had beaten us a couple of weeks earlier in a heart-breaker. Mountain View was closing in on them with time running out. Evon Tseng, the Lynbrook point guard (and ultimate co-MVP of the league), grabbed two key rebounds in the last minute that sealed the win for Lynbrook.

The next day in practice I mentioned to my players that there was a look in Evon's eyes that made it clear she was going to get those rebounds. She simply wasn't going to let Mountain View win the game if she had anything to do with it. I said that we can't control whether the ball goes in the basket. We simply do our best and shoot the ball. But we can control how hard we work to get a rebound. And at the end of our games, we need someone to step up with the kind of determination that Evon demonstrated.

Well, what do you know? In the last several games, Jenny White became our Evon Tseng. She consistently made big plays in the fourth quarter that gave us victories. We held Evon and her teammates in check and defeated Lynbrook. Against Palo Alto, a game that some of you saw, Jenny had key rebounds, steals, and baskets in the fourth quarter. Jenny had been averaging seven or eight turnovers a game. Now she dropped that down to one or two, while handling the ball more.

Against Sacred Heart Cathedral, the final free throws Jenny made came about because she got an offensive rebound and was fouled trying to put it back in. Ultimately we came up short, but that's the way competitive games are. Sometimes you get the bear. Sometimes the bear gets you.

We spent time on a variety of metaphors of leadership last spring. As you all know, I'm especially partial to the leader as coach. Those of you who have coached already know what a thrill it can be. Those of you that haven't had the chance, give it a try when the opportunity presents itself.

Finally, thank you all for being bold enough to try an experimental class and sticking with it through spring-and-fall. And thank you for your interest in my coaching life. The experience has been enhanced by being able to share it with you all. And, if you're in the Bay Area next year, keep an eye on the sports pages for the Women Warriors of Fremont. We'll be back!

Chapter 3

Learning to Love Puerto Rico: Sharing Power with Players

Too many managers don't realize that when you become truly participative, you get into a lot of uncomfortable conversations in which you hear things about the situation and about yourself that you might not like.

—Peter B. Vaill, **Managing as a Performing Art**

One of the hallmarks of the leader as coach (as opposed to a dictator-like leader as "captain of the ship") is the creation of a partnership between players and coach through sharing power and ownership.

In 1968, the *Harvard Business Review* published an article by Frederick Herzberg called "How Do You Motivate Employees?" that was the most requested reprint the magazine has ever published. Herzberg declared that factors that affect workers' job satisfaction fall into two categories, the first of which he referred to as "hygiene" factors. Hygiene factors include such things as pay, working conditions, fringe benefits, and the like.

Herzberg argued that inadequate hygiene factors can *de*-motivate employees but adequate or even outstanding hygiene cannot motivate. That pay is merely a hygiene factor and not a motivator may seem counter-intuitive, but Herzberg explains, "If I get a bonus of $1,000 one year and $500 the next, I am getting extra rewards both years, but psychologically I have taken a $500 cut." A worker may slack off on the job because she is upset about being underpaid. However, while raising her salary may remove a problem, it won't transform her into a highly motivated worker. That requires what Herzberg called "motivators." Motivators include such things as "achievement, recognition for achievement, the work itself, responsibility, and growth or advancement."

Basketball, by its nature, allows for much of what Herzberg labeled motivators. The game is enjoyable, there is ample opportunity for achievement and for being recognized for achievement (although many coaches don't adequately use the tool of recognition), and to learn and grow. What is not so natural about the sport is what he calls "responsibility," but I think is more appropriately referred to as "power."

I am convinced that the most important thing that a coach can do to increase the ownership, commitment, and internal motivation of the members of a team is to develop a partnership with the players. Talk is cheap in this regard. If I want a genuine partnership, I need to share power with my players.

Journal Entry—December 7, 1995

Yesterday was the pits.

We opened the season last Tuesday by meeting our first big milestone. We beat Lynbrook, which had given us so much trouble last year, using our new half-court pressure defense. Our offense was pretty anemic but I was ecstatic that we were able to shut down Evon Tseng, Lynbrook's star point guard, who averaged close to twenty points a game last year. This time we held her to one basket in each of the first three quarters and fourteen points overall.

I was very confident against Los Gatos on Monday. I had seen them play and they had struggled against teams that didn't have a defensive system anywhere near as effective as ours. Well, pride goeth before a fall and I was destined to take a double hit.

We turned the ball over twenty times in the first half alone! We also didn't get back on defense, and LG scored so many fast-break baskets I was almost literally sick to my stomach. Our defensive system depends on all five players sprinting back on defense to get set up. That night we had people jogging down the court and watching black-and-orange jerseys ring the bell time after time. In spite of that, we were in the game for much of it.

Fortunately (I thought), we had the game on tape and I could show the girls how not getting back on defense had killed us. Yesterday I brought my video player to practice and we took a film break. As I pointed out the defensive lapses on the screen, I became angrier and angrier at the lack of effort and hustle I was seeing again. I had trouble keeping a tone of scorn out of my voice as I pointed out individual examples of non-hustle.

As I was reaching a crescendo of vituperation, Jenny said "Well, what about offense? We hardly ever work on offense and the Flex just doesn't work."

I was totally ticked off, more so because the few times they actually ran the Flex they got open shots and usually baskets. So for Jenny to say that the Flex didn't work when they rarely ran it really got to me.

"I don't care about offense. I'm talking about defense. When we learn to play defense it won't matter how we play offense." (Not true, by the way, but I was wound up by then!)

Silence.

Then Shauna, who has more than once earned her honorary title of "coach on the floor," spoke up. "We're pretty frustrated about the offense. I know you want us to focus on defense, but offense is important too and we don't get a chance to work on it in practice so we look terrible in the games."

Then Colleen: "I don't think the Flex is such a good offense. Two years ago when Mr. Kelly was coaching us he always knew which teams played the Flex and we were always able to defend them because we knew what they were going to do, just like Los Gatos knew what we were going to do."

I am so discouraged. I spent a *lot* of time last summer getting up to speed on the Flex. It would be one thing if I had a lot of time to come up with a new offense but we have eight games in the next three weeks. That's very little time to prepare the team for a new offense even if I had the time and energy to come up with one.

However, it was a moment with the potential to be make-or-break for our season. I pride myself on a leadership style that puts a premium on establishing a partnership with my players. I have many times encouraged them to disagree with me rather than sit on their disagreement. I have empowered them and now they feel comfortable using that power. I've created a monster!

I groped for support. I asked some of the players who hadn't spoken yet how they felt about the offense. Chi said in an uncharacteristically quiet voice, "Well, it's kind of hard to make the entry pass." This was a telling point. Many of the turnovers against Los Gatos occurred on the entry pass to the wings. Los Gatos had met our ball handler at the half-court line with a soft double-team and we hadn't done a good job of adjusting to that pressure.

After seeing that the team was united in their distaste for the Flex, I realized I needed to end this meeting before I said something that I would regret. We did a few more conditioning drills and then I sent them home. I wanted to cry! Didn't get much sleep last night.

It is easy to *say* "We're in this together." It is common for coaches to ask for commitment from players without themselves giving up what is pleasurable to have and exercise: the power to have things done the way *you* want them done. If power corrupts—and I think there is no question that it does—then part of the reason it corrupts is because when you have power, you come to *enjoy* the experience of having things done your way. It is no accident that Frank Sinatra's signature song (although actually written by Paul Anka) is "My Way."

Having the power to get things done My Way, the captain's way, can be exhiliarating, and seductive. It is also terribly limiting. It limits the team to being the reflection of the coach.

The seeming paradox is that sharing power *increases* your own power in the sense that the likelihood of success is greater when you create a partnership and truly share power with your players.

Journal Entry—December 8, 1995

Feeling better today. I had lunch with Rich Kelley yesterday. It's nice to have a friend who played for eleven years in the NBA. Initially I was not happy to hear what Rich had to say. He is not a big fan of the Flex. He said it was much more a coach's than a player's offense. Most college and pro teams he knew that tried to use it stopped trying after a period of time. The players just rebelled and refused to run it (does this sound familiar?). He also said it was a "fragile" offense because it depended so much on everyone cutting at exactly the right time. That was the bad news.

The good news is that he had some good ideas about what to do. Rich thinks too many high school coaches overcoach. He advocates a simple approach, for example, liberal use of the pick-and-roll. He pointed out that Karl Malone and John Stockton have relied on it for years. Even though teams know it is coming, they can't stop it consistently. He had seen Colleen and Jenny play and thought they could score a lot of points with it.

This not only made sense to me, but I could actually see how I could design some simple plays that wouldn't take as much time as the Flex for the players to learn. Rich encouraged me to design plays that freed up our best shooters, so the burden of learning the most would be on the players with the most incentive to learn.

I woke up last night about 3, as I usually do during basketball season, and started diagramming a pick-and-roll for Colleen and Jenny, who have been playing together since grade school—almost as long as Stockton and Malone have played together. Since we have gotten into a geographic naming system after our "Iowa" zone offense that was developed by Tom Davis of the University of Iowa, I decided to call our pick-and-roll play "Puerto Rico." See if any of the players can figure it out.

If sharing power is important, how does a coach go about doing it? Sharing power with players is not something a coach necessarily wants to jump into with both feet, particularly if she has a lot of reservations about it. But I am convinced that moving in that direction, giving your players a little more power than feels comfortable at first, will benefit most coaches and teams. Tom Peters once gave one of his high-energy talks at the Stanford Business School that left some of the students perplexed about how to incorporate his "Liberation Management" ideas into their less exuberant management style. I said to them, "If you do exactly what Tom Peters recommends, you'll probably go crazy. But if you go in the direction he is suggesting, a little further than you initially feel comfortable with, my guess is that you'll do pretty well."

Journal Entry—December 9, 1995

They liked "Puerto Rico" immediately. In addition to getting our two best scorers a lot of shots, it begins with downscreens that almost always free up the wings for the entry pass to begin the offense. After practice, I drew up some other new plays. I'm going to name each one after the player who will be the beneficiary: "Hawaii" for Haruka, to free her up beyond the three-point line; "Colorado" for Colleen; "Jamaica" for Jenny.

Journal Entry—December 12, 1995

They liked the new plays too. "Colorado" is especially good for Colleen because it gives her the ball with her face to the basket as she comes across the lane from the weak side. It turns out that she is much more comfortable (and thus better able to score) when she gets the ball in that position than with her back to the basket. Wish I'd known that last year!

The players started asking what the names meant. I told them there was a system, but they would have to figure it out for themselves. Finally a lightbulb flashed. "I know why you named this Puerto Rico. It's because it's a pick-and-roll with a P and an R!" Then flash after flash: "Oh, Jamaica for Jenny." "Colorado, Colleen!" Hawaii, Haruka!"

I've got some new plays to introduce next week: "China" for Chi, "Nigeria" for Natalie. Given that the week began as a nightmare, I'm feeling pretty excited right now. Was it Scarlett O'Hara who said "Tomorrow is another day"?

This chapter describes some ways I experimented with sharing power with my players during my two seasons coaching high school girls' basketball. I am convinced they barely scratched the surface of what is possible. There are three categories of actions I took: (1) I encouraged my players *openly* to disagree with me when they did; (2) I tried to develop individual players as co-leaders of the team; and (3) I shared actual decision making with them.

Let's start with the one that is both the most important and the most uncomfortable for a coach, particularly one who is used to being a captain of the ship.

Encouraging Players to Disagree

One day, while we were working on a full court press, I became frustrated because players wouldn't complete the play and drive to the basket when they stole the ball. Shauna interrupted my tirade by saying "Mr. Thompson, I don't mean to be disrespectful, but the reason we don't finish the play is because you stop us so much that we're never sure when we should keep on going and when we should stop." Oh. . . .

I thanked her for sharing that with me and said that she didn't need to worry about being disrespectful, that I wanted her and her teammates to tell me when they think I'm doing something that isn't working. And then I modified my behavior. I tried to refrain from interrupting the scrimmage or drill until the player who stole the ball completed the play.

One game we were getting hammered by the opposing team. One of the principles I try to live by is to end with a flourish, regardless of the score. As a team, if we can summon up our intensity and play the last part of the game with everything we've got—even, or perhaps especially, in a losing effort—it can lay the groundwork for improvement the next time out. This day we were beaten both physically and mentally. With about four minutes left I called timeout. In the huddle I told the girls, "Look, we're out of this game, but let's end with a flourish. Let's have as much intensity as we can for these last four minutes."

In the locker room during our post-game talk, Chi brought up my "motivational" talk. "Mr. Thompson, I wish you wouldn't tell us things like 'We can't win this game.' It's depressing." I was defensive so I started arguing with her: But you've got to face reality and the score was so-and-so and there was only so much time left and it's important to end with a flourish and blah, blah, blah. Finally I realized what I was doing and stopped. I paused and asked the rest of the team what they thought. Shauna spoke first: "Even if we can't win the game, it's demoralizing to hear you say it." Head nods all around from the rest of the players. From that point on they heard no discouraging word from me, and I realized that we could better focus on giving our best effort for the last few minutes if I didn't hammer them psychologically about the score.

In at least one situation I believe that the fact that my players felt comfortable and able to challenge me directly resulted in a bunch of wins that we would not otherwise have gotten.

During the first games of the 1994–95 season, our full-court press just wasn't working. As much as we worked on it in practice (where it worked quite well against the junior varsity or the second string) it just never seemed to click in a game.

One day in practice I repeatedly criticized Colleen for being so timid, for not playing far enough forward on our press. As much as I had encouraged her to play aggressively, she held back, especially in games. As a result, the other team was often able to make a mid-range pass into the middle and break the press. I was determined to break her of this habit. Finally when she had taken enough, she fired back at me. "If I come up as far as you want me to, the girl behind me will be wide open."

This was an "Aha!" moment for me! All of a sudden I saw what was wrong with our press. We were playing a be-aggressive-or-die defense in an afraid-to-make-a-mistake fashion. We needed to be highly aggressive to force turnovers, but instead were playing to avoid looking stupid if the other team got an easy lay-up. I realized that Colleen wasn't the only one who wasn't as aggressive as I wanted her to be. Virtually everyone was holding back and the result was a press that good teams loved to play against.

My annoyance with Colleen evaporated suddenly as I realized that I hadn't made myself clear. "I'm not worried about the player behind Colleen. If we force the out-of-bounds pass into the corner and then put a strong trap (double-team) on the ball carrier, her only open pass will be to the player behind Colleen. She'll have to make a long pass cross-court with two people in her face. I don't think many players at the high school level can make that play. Even if she does, Colleen may be able to jump up and intercept it. But even if the pass gets by Colleen, the receiver still has to catch the ball with all of you descending on her, and often the biggest player on the other team (who is usually the person the farthest down court) doesn't have the best hands. And then, even if she catches the pass, she still has to make the shot. If we are applying enough pressure, there aren't many teams that are going to be able to make that play on a regular basis.

"If we are as aggressive as I want you to be, we are going to get burned once in a while. In fact, if we don't get burned occasionally, then we probably aren't being aggressive enough. We'll make up for the times they get easy baskets with turnovers and easy baskets of our own. And if a team is able to burn us three or four times in a row, then we probably aren't quick enough to press them and we'll back off. But let's make them prove they can burn us first."

In retrospect, I am even more convinced that this conversation, which addressed the need to take risks and live dangerously with our pressure defense, was the key to our late-season surge in the 1994–95 season. Our press helped us in our CCS first-round victory and, with it clicking, we almost upset heavily favored Sacred Heart Cathedral in our second-round game.

It might never have come together if our players hadn't felt comfortable challenging me. The freedom to challenge me had at least four positive affects.

1. It often forced a clarification of something that I *thought* was crystal clear but actually wasn't. Until the girls really *believed* in what they were doing, the chance of its working weren't very good. So getting clarity on every aspect of what we were trying to do was a big help.

2. More often than I like to admit, a challenge resulted in my seeing that I was off-base in some regard. "This is how I see it, but I might be wrong!" has come to be one of my favorite phrases. A team of yea-sayers might have been more pleasant to coach, but it wouldn't have pushed me to change something that wasn't working. This is important in any activity where it isn't always clear why something is or isn't working. When we lose a game I don't automatically know *why* we lost it or what to do about it. The players' input is crucial for an understanding of what is and isn't working.

3. This is perhaps the most important. By being encouraged to voice their dissatisfaction and speak up, the players felt empowered. Now, in the professional circles in which I move, the word *empowerment* has become almost a cliche. It has been used so much that it has started to lose its linguistic potency. That is a shame, because there is no getting around the incredible effect true empowerment has on an individual or team. Being treated as a person with power is exhilarating. It's fun. It makes you feel like an important person. And it can lead to great efforts on the part of the

empowered, much greater than they otherwise would have made, or even believed they were capable of.

Lack of freedom to disagree with the coach limits a team to being simply a reflection of the personality of the coach. Lynn Frank, my boss at the Oregon Department of Energy, once said to me in his characteristic diplomatic manner, "If you agree with everything I say, why do I need you around?" A good question for every coach to consider.

4. It contributes to alignment of effort, to a team pulling together. Ironically, by encouraging disagreement, a coach is less likely to have passive resistance or outright rebellion from players.

A second cornerstone of the power-sharing strategy is developing players as leaders.

Developing Players as Leaders

Closely tied to the idea of encouraging players to disagree with you is the notion of developing players to play leadership roles on the team (and ultimately in life).

I have been fascinated with leadership development for years. So, it was natural, when I began coaching high school students, that I would explore ways of helping to develop my players as leaders.

Lori Cox, my assistant coach in 1994–95, had an interesting idea about team captains. Lillian and Shelly, the two seniors on the team, were the obvious candidates. Lori suggested that we also select a junior so that there would be continuity of leadership from one year to the next. We finally decided that Shauna was the appropriate person. Shauna was the hardest worker in practice. She was not a great natural basketball talent, but through her hard work and incredible conditioning she had earned a starting position during the preseason practice period. Lori also pointed out that choosing her would help reinforce the message we were trying to send about the importance of hard work. I liked the idea, and so we made Shauna a co-captain; it turned out that she became more of a leader than we could ever have hoped or imagined.

Post-Game Meetings

One of the important tasks of a leader is interpretation of events in a way that keeps the team together and encourages effort in the future. Each game has the potential to *either* increase or decrease future motivation and effort, often in ways that are counter-intuitive. Sometimes a win may have more potential to discourage effort than a loss. We may defeat a weak team and conclude, perhaps subconsciously, that we are so great we don't need to get any better.

In the first game I coached, which took place in the Foothill College summer league in 1994, I was pretty nervous. I wasn't sure what a high school coach did during a game. It looked pretty easy when I had watched others, sometimes pretty critically. Now it didn't seem so simple.

I made it through our first game, which we won (whew!) but then I didn't really know what I wanted to say about it. I knew I wanted to encourage the players to feel good about their potential as a team, but beyond that, the game had moved so fast that I needed time to collect my thoughts. So I asked the team if they had anything they wanted to say about the game. As so often happens, good things came from confusion.

Lillian, a senior and the natural team leader, immediately pointed at a junior (who had not played much the year before and was frustrated with her lack of playing time) and said "She played well." The girl beamed and we went around the circle with each player getting a chance to say something. The players' conclusions were that we had done pretty well for a first game with all the new players. They also had some thoughts about what we needed to work on, including things I hadn't noticed.

I was tickled both because I wouldn't have realized how important it might be to the other girl to be singled out by Lillian, and because I learned a lot from the players' thoughts about our strengths and weaknesses. From that point on I incorporated that ritual into our post-game talks. The players got the chance to talk first, then the assistant coaches, then me.

Once when I was getting a performance appraisal from my boss many years ago, he asked me how I thought I had been doing for the last six months. I felt great about some real breakthroughs I had made with

the group I was managing and told him in great length about my suc-
cesses. He may have wished he hadn't asked me because he already had
my performance review typed and signed—I could see it on the table in
front of him. And what I was telling him didn't match what he had written. I realized that a few minutes later when he gave it to me to read and
sign. I was both disappointed and angry, disappointed that he had not
been aware of all the great things I was doing and angry because he was-
n't likely to change it once he had committed it to paper. Whether it was
a coincidence I don't know, but shortly thereafter we moved to a two-stage
performance appraisal system with a first step in which the person to be
evaluated was asked to write down their accomplishments and areas
needing improvement and share it with the boss. The second, written,
stage came after that and was informed by the discussion in stage one.

One of the reasons I liked having the players comment on the game
first is because there is all kinds of evidence from social-science literature that people's reaction to an event can be colored by what an important "other" has to say about it. This is why there is such a premium on
"spin control" in politics following events like candidate debates. Since
there is no objective measure of who wins such a debate, each side sends
their most highly regarded people out to give a spin, beneficial to their
candidate, to the reporters and commentators who will, in turn, put
their own spin on the event for the mass of voters. Often people who
watch a debate on television without reading or watching any commentators have significantly different views of who won compared to voters
who have been influenced by the pundits.

By having players comment first, I avoided any tendency to have
them simply parrot me, and I often learned a lot that I wouldn't if I had
begun with my own analysis of the game.

Captains' Offsite

Business leaders regularly engage in off-site meetings or retreats in
which the entire management team develops plans for the coming year.
I had done this annually to positive effect with my subordinate managers in the Energy Conservation Division of the Oregon Department of
Energy. I decided to try the same approach with my player-leaders.

During spring 1995 I took Colleen, Jenny and Shauna, co-captains
for the next season, to lunch. I wanted them to meet Leticia Guzman,

who I had asked, pending their approval, to assist me in the next year (Lori Cox had become the assistant womens' coach at De Anza College). I also wanted to encourage them to think of themselves as co-leaders with the coaching staff. I wanted to treat them the way that a businessperson would recruit someone, by discussing it over lunch.

I started by talking about the prospects of our team next year. When I mentioned that I thought we had a chance to end up playing in the CCS (Central Coast Section) Division III championship game, which automatically includes a trip to the NorCal tournament, Shauna let out an "Awesome!"

We talked at length about what the team's goals should be for the next season, the kind of workouts that made sense during the summer, and a variety of other issues. These two hours and the cost of the lunches were as good an investment in leadership development as I made during my coaching career. All three of the captains made major contributions as leaders during the next season, over and above their substantial athletic accomplishments.

Motivational Speeches

I read once about a veteran player for the New York Knicks who took notes every time Pat Riley gave a pre-game pep talk. He was interested in becoming a head coach and wanted to learn from a master. He was amazed to discover that Riley had a different speech for *every* game!

I decided that I would try to emulate Pat Riley in that one respect at least. I had the advantage of having only 24 games for which to prepare motivational talks compared to his 82 (not including the NBA playoffs).

Late in the 1994–95 season, with three games left, I called Jenny, Colleen, and Shauna aside after practice. These three juniors would be co-captains of the team the next season and I wanted them to begin thinking about how they would provide leadership to their teammates next year. I explained to them that we had three conference games left and we needed to win two of the three in order to qualify for the CCS playoffs, something the Fremont Girls had done only once before.

I told the girls that I tried to think of something to motivate the team before each game and I would do that for these three games as well, but that this time I'd like their help. They were going to be captains next year and these games meant the difference between going to CCS or not. I asked each of them to take one of the games and prepare a little talk that would help the team do its best. Colleen immediately said "I'll take Homestead!" which was our next game, and by far the strongest team we played all year.

In the locker room before the Homestead game I gave my little pep talk and then, as I did before every game, I asked if anyone else had anything they wanted to say. Usually this had been met by silence. This time Colleen indicated that she wanted to say something. Since she was sitting with the players facing me, I was able to watch the reaction of her teammates. When she started talking, the eyes of several of the players got very big. This was something new, and she had their total attention.

To my amazement she started talking about how Buster Douglas had been given no chance against Mike Tyson in their heavyweight championship boxing match. But Douglas believed that if he could just keep going back at Tyson and never give up, he could beat him. And he did. When Colleen ended by saying that we needed to go out against Homestead, a team that had soundly trounced us in our first game against them, and just keep going at them like Buster Douglas did, there was total silence in the locker room. It was awesome!

It was also humbling for me. As much pride as I took in my motivational speeches, Colleen's was much better than mine. We ended up losing to Homestead by seven points, significantly better than we had done before (or than almost anyone else had done against them that year). And with Shauna and Jenny responsible for the pre-game inspiration, we won our last two games and qualified for the CCS playoffs.

Leaving the Locker Room

During the 1995–96 season I went a step beyond asking the captains to prepare a motivational talk. In the locker room before the first game in what came to be known as The Streak, I found myself telling the players that we, the coaches, were going to leave them alone in the locker room for a few minutes to talk among themselves about what they needed to do to win this game.

I never did find out what they talked about after we left, but the intensity of our play increased and I attributed some of that to their having the privacy, away from the eyes and ears of the coaches, to say to each other what they felt the need to say. This became a part of our pre-game ritual for every remaining game.

Once Leticia, who often drove Chi home after practices, asked her what went on in the locker room after we left. I suppose she thought that since Chi was the youngest player on the team she might be willing to spill the beans. Chi responded with something like "Wouldn't you like to know!" It was clear to me after that, that the pre-game practice of leaving the team alone to fire each other up (or whatever they did during that time) was an important ritual and one that we as coaches had better keep our noses out of.

The third strategy for sharing power with players was to involve them in decisions that affected the team.

Involving Players in Decision Making

I made a point to involve players in game strategy planning, practice decisions, and scheduling decisions for the next year.

Strategy Plans

Ernie Dossa, whose Homestead High School girls team won the 1996 CCS Division II title, developed three different game plans for the title game with heavily favored Presentation. He laid out all three to his players and asked them to pick the one they wanted to use. The players liked the option that featured a 3-2 zone defense designed to neutralize Presentation's three-point shooters. Ernie agreed and Homestead, much to the surprise of most observers, defeated Presentation for the CCS title.

How much of the value of that strategy came because the players were given ownership of it is an open question, but I believe that their *believing in* and *getting behind* the strategy was at least as important as how good the strategy was in the first place.

In the 1995–96 season we began to use the "Scramble Defense" developed by Jim Larranaga of Bowling Green University. The Scramble is an exciting defense and also a nerve-wracking one for the coach because it requires extreme aggressiveness—even more so than the more standard press we had used the year before. If the players are the least bit timid, the other team will be able to react and get some easy baskets. There are two versions of the Scramble: "thumbs-up," in which the opposing ball carrier is trapped as soon as she comes across the half court line, and "thumbs-down" in which the trap is applied to the player receiving the first pass. We also developed a third option, in which the ball is encouraged or forced down into the corner and the trap is applied there, a difficult place from which to extricate oneself. This variation we called the "Igloo" because an igloo has no corners.

Once we began incorporating the Scramble into our defense, I began asking the team which version they wanted to start in. After a few games Jenny said she thought we should start in thumbs-up because that got everyone pumped up. I realized immediately that she was right. Thumbs-up was the most aggressive of the three options—all five players springing forward toward the mid-court line as the ball carrier approached. The physical act of rushing forward put everyone into an aggressive frame of mind that usually spilled over to the benefit of our rebounding and other aspects of our game. It also seemed to unnerve—and occasionally paralyze—an opposing team. I remember one game in which the opposing coach burned two of his four time-outs in the first two minutes of the game trying to settle his team down, to no avail.

Practice Decisions

Bob Cialdini, the author of *Influence*, a book with a lot to say to coaches, once told me of a technique for reinforcing in young people a positive sense of their personal efficacy. We've all probably heard adults put down young people because their effort or performance wasn't acceptable, and I had a vivid experience of that myself.

Once, when I was visiting some friends, their teenage son offered to do the dishes after dinner. The mother might have thanked him or at least refrained from insulting him, but she responded by saying, "Well, what has gotten into you? This is a miracle, that you would actually *offer* to do the dishes without being asked and nagged. I can't even remember the last time you willingly did the dishes." (I doubt that he volunteered to do them thereafter!) The mother had reinforced the notion in her son's head that he was a shirker who needed to be nagged to do anything productive

But Cialdini saw that this destructive process could be reversed. When a young person does something positive, you can reinforce a positive image in her head. For example, every Friday afternoon as practice wound down I would ask my players if they thought we should practice the next morning.

The decision to practice on Saturday was not one to be agreed to lightly. Because the Fremont gymnasiums were heavily used by a variety of teams and community groups on Saturdays, if we were going to practice we needed to start no later than 8:00 A.M. This was no small matter to players with active social lives that kept them up late on Friday nights.

I always phrased the question in terms of "Would it help the team to practice tomorrow?" Almost always the decision of the players was to practice. Often they would suggest specific things we needed to work on, such as shooting, or mastering our pressure defense, or running our zone offense. The few times when they decided not to do so, they had well-articulated reasons for why it would be better for the team if we took the day off.

Whenever they responded that they'd like to practice, following Cialdini's advice, I would say something like "That's one of the things I like about this team. You are willing to work hard to achieve your goals." This was intended to reinforce their view of themselves as athletes who weren't afraid of hard work and, in fact, even welcomed it.

There always seemed to be a special sense of enjoyment among the team during Saturday practices. Part of that may have been because it seemed pretty cool to be making a sacrifice that most other teams weren't making and partly because it truly was a voluntary sacrifice. They themselves had made the decision to get up early.

Sometime early in the 1994–95 preseason, PBS ran a documentary film about the Stanford Women's Basketball Team called *In the Game*. Jennifer Azzi, one of Stanford's star players (later a member of the U.S. Olympic Team), had a pregame ritual of eating an orange in the locker room. I began bringing oranges to Saturday morning practices as another reminder that this was a special session, something that not every team was willing to do.

Organizing Practices

Mike Dunlap, when he was coaching the California Lutheran University's men's basketball team, used to ask various players to take responsibility for planning and running a late-season practice. He said it invariably was *at least as* hard and intense as the practice he would have designed.

Once, in the locker room after a satisfying victory, I reminded the players to do their visualization in bed that night before they fell asleep. As they cleared out of the locker room, I checked my calendar and discovered that I had an important meeting at work the next day that would keep me from getting to practice on time. The players had left, but Leticia was waiting to walk out with me and I asked her if she would be able to start practice without me. She reminded me that she couldn't be at practice the next day.

I ran ahead to the parking lot and caught Colleen and Jenny. I told them the problem and asked them if they would be willing to organize the first part of practice. I wasn't too worried about the beginning because we had some standard drills and activities that we always began with. They both were more than willing to take charge and I slept a bit easier that night.

The meeting the next day dragged on and then I hit rush-hour traffic, which made the normally 30-minute drive take nearly an hour. I was about an hour and a half late. Something made me pause and look through the window before I entered the gym. What I saw was an incredibly focused and intense bunch of girls, even more focused and intense than usual.

I watched while they did a drill that was not part of our usual practice ritual (they had long ago exhausted those drills). I was interested to see what they would do when they decided they had done this drill long enough, so I waited. When they finished the drill, they huddled briefly and then quickly sprinted to positions and began another drill. After watching this one for a while, and again appreciating how intense they seemed to be, I entered the gym.

I sensed an immediate reduction in intensity. It was almost as if they felt they could relax now because I was there to get after them if they lagged. I almost wished that I had stayed outside for the remainder of the practice.

There is an old saying from Lao-Tzu about the best leader being the one whose absence is not even noticed. If a leader is doing his job, he is preparing his followers to assume leadership. I've always had some ambivalence about this story. As much as I feel uncomfortable in the spotlight, I don't like the thought that I won't be missed if I'm not there. Garrison Keeler once did a bit on his *Prairie Home Companion* radio show about midwestern Norwegian Lutheran men who got embarrassed when they had to stand and walk up to the front of the church to take Communion. Even though everyone else in the church was also in line to get Communion, each man was sure that everyone else in the church was watching him.

Well, I am from Norwegian ancestry and was raised a Lutheran in North Dakota, but I still like to get credit for my leadership. After all, leading people can be a difficult and sometimes unpleasant job, and one of the things that makes it seem worthwhile is having people notice when you are successful.

But, adopting Lao-Tzu's view-point, I took pride in seeing the players organizing such an intense and serious practice in my absence, even as I felt a little uneasy about it.

Scheduling Decisions

Another decision in which I involved players was scheduling for the next year. At the end of each year the coaches in the Santa Clara Valley Athletic League meet to determine which teams will shift between the two divisions. The De Anza Division is for the better teams, the El Camino Division for the weaker teams. We had tied for third in the El Camino Division and I asked the players to advise me about whether to try to move up to the tougher division. I wanted to get an unbiased sense from each person so I tried to keep my own desires out of the discussion. I did stress that if we moved up we would need to make a commitment to work even harder in the off-season so we could compete with the stronger teams.

I encouraged each player to talk about the pros and cons of each option. When it seemed that all the ideas had been thoroughly aired, I asked each player to vote on paper and to sign her name, assuring them I wouldn't tell anyone how they voted. I was surprised that all but one of the players voted to move up. As it turned out, as hard as I argued with my fellow coaches, they narrowly voted that we remain in the El Camino Division.

At that point I was concerned that we wouldn't get the kind of competition we'd need in the conference schedule to be prepared to do our best in the playoffs. So I reviewed with the players my thoughts on scheduling. I told them I'd like to play the toughest pre-conference-season schedule we could and when I outlined my plans they agreed wholeheartedly, with one exception. I was considering dropping out of a tournament because two private schools with outstanding teams had asked us to play them and we couldn't do both. The girls wanted to stay in the tournament and so, even though I regretted not playing these teams, I didn't make that change.

Disruptive Disagreements

One of the byproducts of sharing power with players is that sooner or later you may find them challenging you at a time that is less than ideal. This happened during a timeout in the middle of a CCS playoff game with North Salinas High School. We had fallen behind at the beginning of the game and then had held steady, even gaining a bit, into the third quarter. I wanted to emphasize to our players that we were holding them on defense and if we could just score some points we could still win.

Knowing they hadn't scored many points lately, I asked my score-keeper how many points North Salinas had scored thus far in the third quarter. The student scorekeeper was having trouble figuring that out, which gave one of the players time to cheerfully contribute "What does that matter, Coach?" I ignored her and she repeated "Coach, why is that important?"

I have no doubt that she was trying to be helpful but I could have throttled her at the time because it might have mattered a lot had I gotten the information quickly and been able to use it to show that we were getting better as the game went on. Nonetheless, I like the fact that she felt comfortable speaking out. And I am more than happy with the trade-off of having empowered players who throw themselves with great enthusiasm into the attempt to win at the expense of occasionally having a player sound off when it is not helpful. It is a small price to pay for players that are truly committed to becoming the best they can be.

Second Thoughts

What would I do differently in the future? I'd do more to encourage players to disagree with me. I'd more regularly ask them "What do you think of this?" when introducing a new play or drill, to encourage them to reflect on it. I'd emphasize at the beginning of the season that they will benefit more if they understand why we're doing something and really buy into it. Also, that they will be making a big contribution to the development of the team if they point out ways that we could do something better.

I'd look for more ways to develop players as leaders. I'd try to involve them more in decision making. I'd ask each of the captains, perhaps each of the seniors, to plan a practice session and then I'd sit back and watch it, taking notes on how I might do a better job based on what I saw them do. Then I'd meet with the practice leader afterward to see how she felt about the practice and how she would do it differently next time. I'd avoid offering a lot of criticism but reinforce her for taking this responsibility and carrying it out. Then I'd ask her if she wanted to do another one later in the season. In fact, as I think more about it, I think I'd ask each *junior* to plan a practice, to get them ready for senior leadership.

Finally, I would be much more active in including players in both key and routine decisions. I realize that this can go too far, that often it doesn't really matter what decision you make as long as you make one. It can drive a team crazy to waste time on a decision that doesn't matter much. As management guru Peter Drucker recommends, make reversible decisions quickly and irreversible decisions slowly and carefully. I'd delegate more reversible decisions to them and involve them earlier and more deeply in irreversible ones.

Finally, I might experiment with the notion of having the players vote on the starting line-up. Jeff McKay has had great success with this with the baseball teams he has coached and has encouraged me to try it. He's found that players tend to work harder when they know they have to impress their teammates as well as the coach. Initially I balked at this idea, but in view of how well the other power-sharing arrangements worked, I think I'd try it now.

As much as I did to share power with my players, I feel that I barely scratched the surface of what could be done.

Take-Aways

Sharing Power with Players

1. Go slightly beyond your comfort level in sharing power with your players.

2. Encourage players to disagree with you and then *listen* to them when they do.

3. Recognize that your pronouncements can direct the course of conversation. Get into the habit of asking your players for their ideas and thoughts before you give yours, particularly in postgame meetings.

4. Develop players as co-leaders of the team.
   a. If appropriate, have a younger player as co-captain for continuity of leadership.
   b. Have a special planning session in the off-season for next year's captains.
   c. Ask players to prepare pregame motivational talks for the locker room.
   d. Leave the locker room to allow players to prepare by talking among themselves.

5. Involve players in decisions that affect the team.
   a. Give them options on strategy decisions and ask for their preferences.
   b. Give them the decision on whether to hold optional practices.
   c. Charge key players with designing and running a practice. Then *let* them.
   d. Ask returning players their opinions on scheduling plans for next year.

6. Try out your own ideas on ways to share power with your players.

Chapter 4

Milking the Cow:
The Art of Celebrating Practice

The essence of boredom is to be found in the obsessive search for novelty. Satisfaction lies in mindful repetition, the discovery of endless richness in subtle variations of familiar themes.

—George Leonard, **Mastery**

When my wife was a student at Goddard College in Vermont many years ago, she took a course in agriculture. The course required students to walk several miles from campus to a nearby farm every day, milk a cow, and then walk back. Students complained to the professor that after a few days of doing this, they knew how to milk a cow—so why should they have to continue doing it every day.

The professor said that they only knew how to milk a cow. They hadn't yet learned how to milk a cow *every day* and until they had done that, they hadn't learned what it means to be a farmer.

I am reminded of that story almost every time I consider the issue of practice. Practice can *seem* to be inherently boring. After all, a lot of what practice is is repetition, doing the same thing over and over again. And then repeating it until you can do it right, and then doing it some more to reinforce the habit of doing it the right way. And then doing it some more so you won't forget how to do it correctly, ensuring that you can do it instinctively, on a moment's notice, when needed.

To become really good at almost anything, there is simply no substitute for practice over a long period of time. And to stick with practicing something long enough to master it, there needs to be a high degree of enjoyment, or at least appreciation, of the process of practicing.

Cues of Pleasure

For me there is something sensorily rich about being in a gym in which young people are playing basketball. Perhaps the hardest part of my job coaching was getting to the gym every day. I have a challenging and enjoyable job that requires me to be available to interact with a large number of MBA students every day. It is not unusual for me to have five or more conversations with students on my way to my car at the end of a day. These conversations are not niceties. They are part of how I do my job.

So, each day I found it a challenge to leave work in time to get to the gym for the beginning of practice. Often as I drove to Fremont High School I became aware that I was irritated at the stress of having to juggle my many activities. However, once I got to the gym and opened the door, the irritation melted away and I felt a rush of excitement.

This reminded me of George Leonard's description in his book *Mastery,* of how a writer friend felt about the place that he did his work.

> As soon as I walk into my study, I start getting cues of pleasure—
> my books on the shelves, the particular odor of the room. These
> cues begin to tie into what I've written and what I'm about to
> write. Even if I've stayed up all night, my fatigue disappears, just
> like that. There's a whole range of pleasure waiting for me, from
> making one sentence work to getting a new insight.

One of the biggest cues of pleasure I got from coaching was the sound of basketballs—bammetta, bammetta, bammetta—hitting the floor. Often when I arrived at the gymnasium, the baskets had been raised to the ceiling earlier in the day. I got an unreasonable sense of enjoyment from shooting a basketball as each basket slowly descended from the rafters. I was challenged to get exactly the right amount of lift and angle off the glass so as to be able to score. The sense of accomplishment I felt when I was able to hit several in a row was quite out of proportion to the value of such a skill. I loved watching the players shoot layups. I liked the moments of quiet communication that were possible during their stretching exercises. It was a time to share with them what I hoped to get done that day in practice and find out what was on their minds. I even liked the daily setting up of scoreboard and time clock we used for certain ritual drills. This required pulling out a section of the bleachers, which initially was a bit of a nuisance. Over time I even came to enjoy the process of pulling the bleacher out at a steady pace, not too quickly, not too jerkily (or else it would stick). Then, stooping beneath the bleachers to plug in the cables for the scoreboard and time clock. The buzzing sound that the scoreboard clock made every day when I flipped the switch on the fuse box was like music.

I was aware of time passing every day that I coached. I knew that the season would end before we knew it, that Lillian and Shelly (and the next year, Haruka, Jenny, Amalia, Colleen, Shauna, and Karen) would soon be graduating and no longer part of the daily rituals. I knew it would end all too quickly and that was going to be a sad day.

There was, simply, no other place I would rather have been at those moments.

Journal Entry—October 1994

George McCown, founder of the buyout firm McCown De Leeuw & Co. and Chairman of the World Business Academy, spoke in Learning to Lead the other day. He captivated the students (and me as well) with his stories of turning around companies in trouble. He had some interesting personal advice for the students about the importance of habits. He said that if you are going to be successful you need to develop good habits. Now that's nothing new, but he added an angle that was intriguing to me. He said that you need to get about 80% of your life running routinely by force of your habits so that you can devote your creative energy to the 20% that really requires out-of-the-box thinking. Spending creative energy on the routine stuff means you're not going to be hitting on all cylinders when you come up against the tough issues.

This reminded me of Ted Sizer's comment: "Show me a quarterback who thinks and I'll show you a losing team." Initially I was uncomfortable with it, but much of what an athlete needs to do in a game should have been practiced so many times that it becomes instinctive (or habitual!). Then creativity can be released to work in those intense situations when opportunities present themselves to the mind that has learned to be free to focus on them. There are some lessons here to be applied to how I run basketball practice, I'm sure.

Where We Spend Our Lives

I was listening to Talk of the Nation Science Friday on NPR one morning. The topic was how sports psychology and technology are used by Olympic athletes in their training. One of the experts commented that, until recently, sports were seasonal, with the season lasting about three months. Then athletes would find something else to do with their recreational time. This has changed, with most world class athletes practicing year round. He said, in classic understatement, "These athletes practice a lot, most of them seven days a week."

Practice is where athletes spend their lives. The focus is on preparing for a contest or series of competitions, but the act of competing is a very small percentage of the total time. Even for less-than-world-class athletes, the ratio of practice time to game time is a minimum of six to one. As such, practice needs to be valued not just for what it can produce, such as a winning performance, but as time that is precious in itself, irrespective of outcome.

Often when I find myself so goal-oriented that I forget to enjoy the normal, practice-like moments that are where I spend my life, I am reminded of a haunting poem by Mary Jean Irion.

        NORMAL DAY - -

Let me be aware of the treasure you are.
Let me learn from you, love you, savor you, bless you
before you depart.

Let me not pass you by in quest of some perfect
tomorrow. Let me hold you while I may,
for it will not always be so.

One day I will dig my fingers into the earth
or bury my face in the pillow or stretch myself taut
or raise my hands to the sky

and want more than all the world: your return.

Wasted Moments

Years ago someone described to me how we waste most of our moments. He gave this example. When he is hungry, he gets up from his chair and walks to the kitchen to see what is in the refrigerator. He opens the door of the refrigerator and eyes the selections. He finally chooses something and takes it out. He then does whatever he needs to do to prepare the food—peels an orange, pours a glass of liquid, heats some soup. Finally he puts teeth and lips and tongue to the sustenance.

Of all the moments that he just described, he values only the final one in which he eats or drinks the food or liquid. The other moments are not valued for themselves, for the irreplaceable gifts that they are, but are hurried through to get to the prized moment of tasting the treat.

Now I love the pageantry and excitement of a basketball game as much as the next person. And the reality of an upcoming game against a worthy opponent gives an intensity to practices that is unlikely to occur in its absence. When the whistle blows and the ball is tossed in the air, the experience is as delectable as the first bite of a sweet orange.

But I also want to value the moment in which I get up out of the chair and the moment in which I walk to the kitchen and the moment in which I open the refrigerator door. I want to value the moments in practice as much as the moments in games. Each moment is a part of my life that, once passed, will never return. And I suspect the warm glow of memory may linger longer on those moments of practice than the more glittery ones of games. Certainly, writing this book I am struck by how many specific moments of practice come storming into my thoughts.

Journal Entry—October 8, 1995

Last week was the first week of pre-season workouts. Eric Reveno called me last week. He recently became director of a nonprofit organization called Riekes Center for Human Enhancement, founded by Gary Riekes to help young people reach their potential through a variety of means, including athletics. I often used Eric as a role model for my players before I ever met him. As a rabid Stanford hoops fan, I watched Eric's progress year-by-year. The year after he had back surgery he came back to action as a vastly improved player. He developed a deadly move from the left side of the key in which he turned and fell away to his left with a shot that was virtually unstoppable. I told my players about Eric as an example of what is possible in the off-season. Each player has the chance to come back next year with something totally new to add to her game.

Then Eric showed up at the GSB after a few years of playing basketball and working in Japan. He signed up for Learning to Lead and we've kept in touch since.

He called me a while back to have lunch and tell me about his new venture. He made the mistake of mentioning that he was working with the Palo Alto High boys basketball team as a trial run. I immediately accused him of sexism unless he also worked out with a girls team. I just happened to know one that would be interested. I didn't have to twist his arm much, which is good because he is a very strong fellow.

Eric ran the girls through some intriguing conditioning drills during the first few days, using harnesses and other exotic equipment that made the hard work of getting into shape more interesting.

Later in the week, Eric wasn't able to make our workout session so he sent Kate Paye, who's working with him this summer. When the girls discovered that Kate Paye, star of the Stanford women's basketball team, was there, they were beaming!

The players should have sore mouths tomorrow, what with all the grinning and giggling from the excitement at spending the day with Kate Paye. I told Eric later that it's always nice for me to see him but, frankly, since he played only with the Stanford *men's* team my players would just as soon see Kate Paye. At one point I took a picture of Shauna working on the harness with Kate. She is straining to hold onto Kate with all of her physical might while unable to suppress an ear-to-ear grin!

The Will to Win Revisited

Bobby Knight was once quoted as saying "The will to win is overrated as a means of doing so. What is important is the will to *prepare* (emphasis added) and the ability to execute."

I agree. In most cases it is nonsense to think that a person can simply will themselves to do something they've never done before without having prepared themselves physically and mentally to do so. A person who completes a marathon doesn't do it by sheer willpower in the moment. She has exercised her will to *prepare* by running lots of miles for many months. The many small acts of will power *in preparing* make it possible to execute in the moment of the marathon.

Taking this to the wider world of work, any time I see someone who does a nice job with a sales presentation or running a meeting or giving a speech, I can usually be pretty confident that I am seeing only the tip of the iceberg. Before I began to give a lot of presentations, I remember being amazed when Fred Miller, then director of the Oregon Department of Energy, told me he spent four to five hours preparing for every presentation. Before I ever taught a class at the Stanford Business School, I remember being skeptical of professors who claimed to spend 10 or more hours preparing for every hour in the classroom. Not any more. I now know from personal experience the rude ratio of secluded practice to spotlighted performance.

During the 1996 Summer Olympics I read that swimmer Janet Evans, who was retiring after this last competition, said she was already beginning to miss her time in the pool practicing. I think for most people to be able to maintain a commitment to practice, with the necessary intensity over a long enough time to excel in anything, there has to be an element of celebration in practicing. For most of us, the will to prepare requires that we experience a large element of joy in the process of practicing.

Natalie Goldberg, in *Writing Down the Bones*, captured the delight one can develop for practicing:

> . . . Some days you don't want to run and you resist every step of the three miles, but you do it anyway. You practice whether you want to or not. You don't wait around for inspiration and a deep desire to run. It'll never happen, especially if you are out of shape and have been avoiding it. But if you run regularly, you train your mind to cut through or ignore your resistance. You just do it. And in the middle of the run, you love it. When you come to the end, you never want to stop. And you stop, hungry for the next time.

Goldberg was thinking about writing while writing about running, but it holds for just about anything. The bottom line for a coach (or teacher or manager or . . .) is that the art of celebrating practice is a crucial element of success.

Journal Entry — November 30, 1995

The other day Chi and Natalie came to me at the beginning of practice and asked if they might be excused early from practice. It turned out it was Colleen's birthday and they had gotten a cake and soda to celebrate. They wanted me to pretend that they had some reason to be excused early so they could go into the coaches' office and get the cake ready. I made a big production of getting everyone lined up for liners and then said "Wait, I forgot, we need to have a team meeting in the coaches' office." Then when the players filed in Chi and Natalie squirted that string stuff that comes out of a can like aerosol all over Colleen. After everyone had cake and soda, someone asked if we still had to go back to the gym and do liners. I said, no, we could miss them this once.

I was pleased at the leadership that Chi and Natalie showed in doing this, since celebrating milestones is an important part of team building. I complimented them both afterward, saying that they had demonstrated leadership by doing that. Chi couldn't resist getting in a dig by saying "Hey, yeah, you're the coach. You should be doing this!" I told her I couldn't begin to match her style in throwing parties.

Playing Like You Practice

It has been said that great teams play like they practice, which means that you need to learn to practice like you want to be able to play. I must have said that to my players several thousand times during the last two years.

To me, practicing the way you want to play required a balancing act of sorts. We wanted a level of intensity that was abnormal in regular life. We wanted to concentrate on what we were doing so that we could make the most of every minute together on the court. There was simply so much to learn and rehearse, that we just weren't going to get where we needed to be if we took a laissez faire attitude at practice.

At the same time, I never wanted the players to lose sight of how much fun basketball was. It wasn't brain surgery or pulling someone out of a burning building. It was a recreational activity, albeit one at which we wanted to excel. So finding the balance point between intensity and enjoyment was a constant challenge.

Drills with Consequences

One of the reasons that games tend to be more intense than practices is because games have consequences. Not only is there the consequence of losing the game, but it is also entirely possible to be embarrassed by your opponent. The latter also may be true in a practice but the audience is much smaller.

So it makes sense that if you want to practice like you play you need to introduce consequences into practice. This is another area in which I am indebted to Mike Dunlap for sharing his insights with me. He taught me to conduct practices by the time clock and scoreboard wherever possible and to have a consequence for every drill. He further shared with me the insight that the consequence needn't be large. In fact, it often worked better if the consequence were small. His preferred consequence was five push-ups.

We began doing drills in pairs in which the slower runner, or less accurate shooter, or less aggressive rebounder paid the price. The great thing about the push-up consequence is that it doesn't take much effort or time, and doesn't leave a residue of negativity in the players who experience it. Five push-ups isn't much but none of the girls wanted to be the ones hitting the floor at the end of the exercise. The consequence added just enough of an edge to the drill to increase the intensity without a spillover of noxious negativity that might serve as a lingering irritant to distract the losing players from concentrating on the next drill, which is important because there is never enough time to practice everything as fully as a coach would like.

When I was coaching younger kids and we had two one-hour practices a week, I would dream about what it must be like to be able to practice every day. But even with practicing two to three hours every day, I almost always felt that I needed just a little bit more time at the end of the practice preceding a game. So, having a consequence that can be consumed quickly and completely so as to get on to the next activity is important.

With competitive folks, it doesn't take much to get them fired up and it's easy to overdo it so that competition tears at the fabric of teamwork. The Stanford Business School has a reputation as a cooperative place compared to other business schools. I think the genius in that is that when you have highly competitive people, as most Stanford MBA students are, you get better results by encouraging cooperation. The competition, though muted, is still there and working the kind of magic that competition works. For us, five push-ups did the job, and every drill that we applied that consequence to had just enough of an edge to make it more game-like.

Developing a Taste for the Distasteful

One of the lessons I learned from my first year of coaching was that I needed to emphasize rebounding more in my second year. When Tara VanDerveer spoke in Learning to Lead, she surprised me by saying "Offense entertains fans. Defense wins games. Rebounding wins championships."

I thought I knew that phrase but I had heard only the first two sentences. After my first year coaching I was a believer. When we lost, it was generally because the other team out-rebounded us. In almost every pregame conference when the referees asked me if I had any concerns, I said "We have a skinny team and we work really hard at blocking out. But in some games when the referees (those bad *other* referees, never you two distinguished gentlemen!) don't call over-the-back we have a hard time competing with big beefy teams."

It almost never helped. I learned after a while that the more aggressive team got the benefit of the doubt from most referees. That may be partly because most of the referees were men and were used to boys' games, which are far more physical than the girls' games. It may also be because the more aggressive team was usually the better team, and in high school basketball, like the NBA, talent has its privilege. And maybe, as Rich Kelley liked to rib me, the refs usually don't like coaches who are whiners!

Eventually I told my players that they could not expect any help from the referees. If they called an over-the-back against the other team, consider it a gift. But in general we needed to block out so strongly that the only way the other team could go over the back to get a rebound would be to knock us down.

In reflecting on what we needed to do differently the second year, rebounding was at the very top of my list. I determined that we would devote much more practice time to rebounding. As it turned out, we *still* didn't spend as much time on it or emphasize it as much as we needed to. Part of the problem is that rebounding is distasteful to most people.

The players would block out when we did specific rebounding drills. However, as soon as we scrimmaged, all memory of blocking out seemed to evaporate from their heads. Finally in frustration I stumbled on a method that worked better, something I call the "Delayed Zap."

I divided players into teams of approximately equal ability. We scrimmaged for a given period of time (say, ten running minutes on the scoreboard clock). The losing team would face the standard push-up consequence. But in this drill, *every* time there was a shot and the defending team failed to have at least one person (later two) block out their opponent, they would have to do an additional set of push-ups. Thus a team could win the game (in terms of baskets scored) but still end up doing lots of push-ups if they consistently failed to block out.

I was amazed how quickly people started looking around for someone to put a body on. Blocking out is a distasteful activity for most players (part of the reason Dennis Rodman is such a successful rebounder is that he seems to actually *like* the process of banging bodies and blocking out), but they took to this drill with vigor once they realized that the lack of blocking out would have a delayed deleterious effect.

Nonetheless, as the season wore on, for some reason I reduced the amount of time spent on rebounding drills. We introduced more and more things as the season went on and the amount of time for practice remained the same. I may also have subconsciously worried that someone would get hurt because our rebounding drills tended to be ferocious affairs. And perhaps I need to face the fact that I find rebounding distasteful and need to develop my own taste for it as a coach.

All I can say is that if I coach again, I will redouble the amount of time and energy I expend on getting the team to be tenacious rebounders who refuse to be denied.

Journal Entry—January 17, 1996

Yesterday Ron Rossi came to watch practice and, as usual when we have observers, I roped him into some drills. At the end we did some shooting contests, coaches against the players. We did a three-point shooting contest and argued for some time about what the conseqence should be. Finally we agreed that the losers would have to get down on their knees and bow low three times to the winners while saying "We are not worthy." Given that the JV team was practicing at the other end of the gym, there was a lot of intensity in the contest. *No one* wanted to have to do that in front of the younger players. Ron, Leticia, Annie, and I ended up losing and the varsity players screamed and shouted at the JV players to watch us as we prostrated ourselves. It was quite a moment. I was glad the coaches lost because we aren't the ones who have to play a game tomorrow night.

Practicing Timeouts

We even practiced our timeouts. I had became frustrated by how much time we wasted in our timeout huddles when there wasn't that much to begin with. Some players immediately went for their water bottles. Some looked for a towel. It seemed that almost every other comment I made was aimed at getting everyone's attention rather than focusing on what we needed to do on the court.

Finally I decided that we needed to practice appropriate timeout behavior. The players thought this was pretty funny. I had five people out on the floor and the rest sitting on chairs as if they were in a game. When I called timeout, I had them run over to the bench. I told the players who were being subbed in that they needed to go to the person they were replacing and tell them that they were in for them. I wanted the five people who were going to be on the court when we broke from the huddle to be seated close together with the rest of the team standing in a semi-circle.

They laughed and had fun with this, but they also got the message and our huddle discipline improved 100% from then on. I believe it made the difference in more than one game.

Drills Under Pressure

I am going to reveal something that some people won't want to hear. I once bought a Bobby Knight videotape. Some of my friends who are fellow practictioners of the discipline of positive coaching don't want me to admit this because of Mr. Knight's, shall we say, *authoritarian* style of leadership.

But I knew that he has a reputation for organizing practices that are more challenging than game situations. I wanted to know what some of those techniques were so I bought the tape, watched it several times and incorporated ideas from it into my own practices. Perhaps the most valuable idea was to conduct drills in practice under conditions more chaotic and pressure-filled than is likely to happen in a game situation.

From then on we did our shooting drills with multiple shooter-rebounder-passer trios at each basket. Initially the players asked why they couldn't spread out since we had other baskets that weren't being used. I explained that the chaos that resulted from having three players simultaneously shooting at the same basket would make a game situation in which you were the only shooter seem tame by comparison. They understood that and came to value the close quarters.

We also scrimmaged with more than ten players. For example, when we prepared for a team that was known for its defensive pressure, we scrimmaged five-on-seven with the two extra defensive players having a green light to double-team anyone they chose at any time. This did two things. It gave our starters experience with being double-teamed. It also compensated for the fact that our starters were more talented than the second team. Five-on-five, the starters would usually be able to have their way with the second team. Five-on-seven required that they play as hard as they could to emerge victorious.

Getting Comfortable with Discomfort

George Leonard notes ". . . Learning almost any skill involves certain indignities. Your first few dives are likely to be belly flops—and they'll draw the attention of almost everyone at the pool. Are you willing to accept that? If not, forget diving."

One of the most basic (and most easily forgotten) lessons is how uncomfortable it is to learn a new skill. A student in my Learning to Lead class shared the four stages of mastering a new skill that he learned in a public speaking class.

The first stage is *unconscious incompetence*. You aren't very good at something but it has never been called to your attention. You may be living in a dream world in which you think you are good at something but you're wrong! I refer to this as being "fat, dumb and happy."

When you begin consciously to try to change or learn a new skill, you enter into the most uncomfortable stage, that of *conscious incompetence*. You aren't any worse than you were before, but now you are aware of it. You're still fat and dumb, but you're not happy any more. Learning to Lead involved lots of feedback for students on their performance as leaders. Each week I e-mailed the students who were the assigned leaders of their "evening learning teams" that week to see how the meeting went. I received the following e-mail from a student following her turn as leader.

> I know that this is all a learning process, but I was still frustrated with my own performance. I've never thought this much about leading before—I always just did it. Maybe I wasn't very good at it before, but it was certainly less painful than this whole process. I do want to improve. Every now and again, though, I'm just not sure what to do next. Sorry for ending on a down note—it's just that I think I've been constructively criticized once too many.

This is a perfect example of someone in stage two, in some degree of pain at becoming aware of how far she is away from the idealized picture she had in her head of herself as a leader.

The third stage is *conscious competence*. This is where you can perform the skill properly if and when you maintain mental concentration. This can be exhausting, mentally more than physically.

And finally, if you stick with it, you reach the point where you can perform without a lot of focus. You have internalized the move or skill to the point where it seems "natural." This is the stage of *unconscious competence* and it is very rewarding.

One of my goals was to get my team to master the complexities of an aggressive pressure defense. I shared the four stages with my players. I told them that the first step is to know in your head what needs to be done. Then there is being able to do with the body what is known in the head in a controlled environment in practice. Next is doing it in a situation in which the outcome matters, such as an important game. This is often a matter of *remembering* to do it when there are all kinds of distractions. And finally there is the quite advanced stage of being able to both remember and execute it when you are tired. As someone once said, "Fatigue doth make cowards of us all."

We worked all season long in 1995–96 on a pressure defense that depended on denying the obvious next pass all over the court and applying intense pressure on the opposing ball carrier. More often than I would like, we simply "forgot" or at some level decided it was too risky or we were too tired to do it late in a game.

When we finally "got" it, in both a mental and an even-when-fatigued physical sense, we embarked on our season-ending streak (see Interlude: "The Streak"). Wondrously, the fatigue melted away as we began to enjoy the physical effort of unconscious competence.

I found that sharing with my players how the new skill-development process worked helped them deal with the inevitable discomfort. It helped them to know that learning a new skill virtually requires that you feel uncomfortable, but that the discomfort is nothing more than a stage that will pass. Knowing the discomfort was unavoidable (if you were to grow) and that it is temporary is a big relief when you are in pain.

Ritual Activities

One of the benefits of daily practice is that you have the opportunity to create rituals that players come to look forward to. Among our ritual drills, the one that our team came to love the most was what we called the "Stanford Drill."

The Stanford Drill is a complex full-court passing and shooting drill at a break-neck pace, with players covering a lot of ground in a short time and taking a lot of shots from a variety of spots on the floor. One day, early in my first season of coaching, I took several of my players to watch the Stanford women's team practice. Tara VanDerveer was introducing a new drill, so I took notes. I was intrigued to see that the drill was complex enough that it took even the Stanford players, known for both their intelligence and their basketball ability, quite a few times through before they could run it without a hitch. I tried it with my players at our next practice. They liked it partly because because they worshipped the Stanford women's team and partly because it was a lot of fun. From a coach's viewpoint it also had the advantage of forcing players to get off shots quickly after having run the length of the floor in a game-like, fast-break situation.

After we got the hang of it, I started setting the clock for six minutes and keeping track of every basket on the scoreboard. Over time we im-

proved our execution of the drill and began to score more and more baskets in the six minutes. It was interesting to see the evolution of my players' understanding of what was needed to excel in the drill. At first Chi
would begin to call attention to the amount of time left when the clock
got down to one minute. The intensity would pick up noticeably in that
last minute as the players tried to make sure that every possible basket
was shot and made.

In short order they began to understand that to break their own
record they would need to execute the drill with intensity the entire six
minutes. They couldn't coast for five minutes and then get intense the
last minute and reach a new high.

In year one we set a new team record with something like 82 baskets
just before the end of the regular conference season. Then we brought up
five junior-varsity players to join the team for the playoffs. We continued
to run the Stanford Drill with the new players, and, as would be expected,
the performance went way down. Over the two weeks that we practiced
with the expanded squad we gradually improved, until the new enlarged
team broke the previous record in spite of the lower skill and experience
level of the new players. This was a delightful sign that the veterans had
welcomed the younger girls onto the team and that the two groups had
quickly merged as a new high-performance team.

Conversation as a Practice Ritual

The relationship between talking and action is an interesting one. Karl
Weick has a provocative interpretation of Norman Maclean's book *Young
Men and Fire*, an account of a terrible fire that occurred in August 1949 at
a remote site in Montana called Mann Gulch. A group of sixteen "smoke
jumpers" parachuted into a conventional-looking fire, only to be trapped
when the fire turned on them. Thirteen of the sixteen were killed.
Perhaps the most haunting part of the tragedy was that many of the
young men died because they didn't realize the significance of their
leader's action in setting an escape fire. They ignored his motioning to
them to lie down in the burning area and were quickly overtaken by the
rampaging fire; he could only watch from safety as they perished.

Weick argues for conversation being a critical element in any
group's ability to respond quickly in an emergency-like situation.
"Evidence is growing that nonstop talk is a crucial source of coordina-

tion in complex systems that are susceptible to disasters." The fact that each of the young men was trained was largely irrelevant. The more salient feature was that the group was newly formed and had not had the opportunity through extensive conversation to get to know and trust each other and their leader's judgment. When he asked them to do something that didn't make sense they ignored him—to their misfortune.

About a third of the way through a typical practice session, usually following a set of free throws, we would gather on the bleachers to talk. We would talk about the upcoming game, about individual and team goals that we had set for ourselves, about something I had read since the last practice, what we were going to do the remainder of practice, or whatever was on people's minds.

Sometimes I would give the players index cards and ask them to respond to questions in writing. Once late in the season I asked them to rate the team's performance on a scale of 1 to 10, their own performance by the same scale, and what they believed they needed to do to help the team have the very best ending to the season we could have. All but one player rated the performance of the team higher than their own.

This reminded me of a marriage counselor I once read about who developed a quick diagnostic tool he used for couples who came to him for help in getting their relationship back on track. He asked each person privately "Who gives the most to this relationship, you or your spouse?" Often both individuals will say that they give more than their partner and that's the problem! This was not a good sign that the marriage could be saved.

Every once in a while, the counselor would find a couple in which both partners would say that their partner contributed more to the relationship than they did! These are the relationships blessed by grace, and almost always the couples were able to get their marriages back on track.

I took my players' responses to mean that they felt better about the contributions of their teammates than their own, which is a pretty good place for a team to be. Each of them is likely to try harder to improve their performance without having a lot of gripes about how hard their teammates are working. Like the married couples, a team with most of its players feeling this way is in pretty good shape.

I had been influenced by coaches who stressed the importance of getting the most out of every minute of practice, so initially I organized practices filled with drills, while keeping any conversations short and sweet. Over time I came to realize that conversation was not a distraction but an important part of practice, as important in its way as shooting or defense or conditioning. These conversations were where we came together as a team and were among the most valuable moments in our practices.

Life's Simple Pleasures

Year's ago when I was a kid, Dairy Queen had a television commercial in which a little boy and his dad went to get a cone on a hot day. The theme was "one of life's simple pleasures." Basketball practice contained hundreds of moments of simple pleasures whenever I was present and at peace enough to notice them. One of my favorite moments grew out of our ritual free-throw shooting. We always shot after running or scrimmaging so the players would shoot when tired, as in a game. Each player took ten or twenty shots, keeping track of their "makes." When everyone had finished we would gather on the bleachers and I would ask each player how many they made. I put their number of makes up on the scoreboard. When I had all the makes on the scoreboard, we turned to Haruka, who had the ability to divide any two numbers in her head and give the results as a shooting percentage in a nanosecond. It was one of my life's small pleasures to watch Haruka scrunch up her face in a brief frown of concentration before telling us our team's free-throw shooting percentage.

Take-Aways

The Art of Celebrating Practice

1. Celebrate the act of practicing. Literally celebrate birthdays and other special events. Learn (and teach your players) to value practice for itself, not just for what it may lead to (victory in a game). Encourage your players to enjoy every "normal day" in practice.

2. Develop a set of rituals that you and your players can look forward to each day at practice. The ideal ritual would be enjoyable while contributing to development of good habits that will serve you well in games.

3. Recognize the value of "team conversation." Make conversation a ritual part of each practice. Plan what you want to cover in the conversation with the same degree of thoughtfulness you do the physical drills.

4. Discuss the importance of preparation with your players and the need to be committed to preparing so as to be able to execute when the time comes. Tell them about the four stages of skill development and reassure them that discomfort is inevitable and also that it passes.

5. Develop consequences for as many drills as possible. Make the consequences short and snappy and no more than slightly unpleasant. Use the timer and scoreboard to add intensity to drills.

6. Use the concept of the "Delayed Zap" to encourage players to develop a taste for the distasteful, such as blocking out for rebounds. Get the team to buy in to the use of the Delayed Zap and even solicit from them the situations in which it makes sense to use it.

7. Enjoy the simple pleasures that will come your way every day!

Dark December

December 1995 was as tough a month as I have ever known. *

Journal Entry—December 17, 1995

I am beginning to wonder about my coaching ability. Still haven't won a game at Cupertino High School. Last year when we lost all three games in the Cupertino Tournament I never dreamed it would happen again this year. We lost to a terrific Prospect team in the opener. I thought we might be able to play with them, and we did for a while, but eventually we couldn't handle their constant pressure. Then we lost to a Mt. Pleasant team that we should have been able to beat. But the bottom was still ahead. We ended up playing Cupertino in the double loser's bracket. We bumbled around in the first half and finally pulled ahead 36–32 at the end of the third quarter. With a handful of minutes left we had the game comfortably in hand until I screwed up. I thought Colleen had three fouls, so was stunned when she picked up her fifth and left the game with three minutes left. Then I also miscounted our timeouts and had none left to calm us down in the final minute when we couldn't keep Cupertino from scoring every time they got the ball. We ended on the short end of a 49–48 score. I told the girls at practice today that I wasn't coaching very well and that I wasn't going to shave again until I felt that I was coaching up to my abilities. I feel so terrible about how I've been coaching that I need to do something to make myself suffer. I hate the feel of a beard, so the constant irritation may serve as a reminder to get positive and focused. We'll see.

*See Chapter 3, page 2, for journal entry on our first game of the season against Los Gatos.

Journal Entry—December 26, 1995

Came home after the Homestead game to find my stepfather, Orville, in bed and pretty much out of his head. We called the ambulance, which took him to El Camino Hospital. He had a blocked kidney caused by scar tissue built up from radiation treatment after his colostomy a decade ago. It almost killed him. The morning after he was admitted, the doctor asked us if we wanted them to use extraordinary means to revive him if his heart stopped during his operation. I almost shouted "You bet we do!" The doctor was worried about the combination of the infection in his blood, the danger of fluid going to his lungs, and his low, low blood pressure. Fortunately the antibiotic knocked out the infection and no fluid got into his lungs. He's going to make it, thank God.

This whole experience helped me remember, at least for a little while, how artificial the obsession with winning basketball games really is. And I needed that after the way we played against Homestead. We went scoreless in the first quarter (nothing, none, nil, nada, zero, zilch, zippo, zed, the empty set, a big black hole) and trailed 22–4 at half time. Homestead is a great team, but I really think we have the ability to play with them—although you'd never know it from this game. Not having Natalie also hurt because she is so fast and can break a press virtually by herself.

Journal Entry—December 30, 1995

There is an old Chinese proverb to be careful of what you wish for because you might get it. I wished to get my team into the Mitty Tournament—and now I understand the proverb in a new and painful way.

I attended the Mitty tournament last year and decided that was where we should be playing. Many of the top local teams, usually including at least one from the Los Angeles area, were there. College coaches attended because there were so many good players to scout. I thought Colleen and Jenny might have the potential to play college ball if they kept improving and I thought it was possible they would get some attention. In addition, it was really exciting, with lots of teams and big crowds—at least for the evening games, which featured the winners' bracket teams.

So I started bugging the Mitty tournament director as soon as the season ended to give us the spot that I knew was going to be open (a coach I know was leaving the tournament because so many of his players were gone on vacation right after Christmas). That should have been a warning to me. . .

As soon as I got word from Mitty that we were accepted into the tournament, I wrote a letter to all the returning players and their parents asking them to try not to schedule vacation for the days immediately following Christmas when the tournament took place. I immediately got a call from the Natalie's father saying that they had planned a trip to Hong Kong for Christmas. He was very concerned about her missing the tournament and I had the notion that, if I had asked him to, they would trade in their tickets so she wouldn't miss the tournament.

Not realizing how important Natalie was going to be to the team, I told Natalie's dad that would be fine. Thinking no news was good news, I was relieved that no other players or parents called. Silly me.

In November I got the schedule for the Tournament and discovered that we would face Sacred Heart Prep in the first round on Thursday morning to open the tournament. This was both a depressing thought and a great honor. Sacred Heart Prep, a Division V school, is the defending Division I state champion. They don't figure to be quite as good as last year, with two graduating players having gone on to Division I college teams, but still are one of the top teams in the state.

The depressing part was that we were going to get crushed, even if Natalie were there. The honor was in simply being on the same floor with such a strong and well-coached team. I am reminded of the player from a small country's Olympic basketball team who had a teammate take his picture guarding Michael Jordan. This player smiled into the camera as Jordan slipped around him for a basket. He didn't have any illusions about being able to stop Jordan, but he was certainly going to enjoy telling his children and grandchildren about the time he guarded Michael Jordan, and he'd have the photo to prove it!

When I got the schedule I was excited to tell the team about getting to play SHP. I was especially glad that Colleen would have a chance to play against SHP because she had been injured the summer before when we played them in Foothill's summer league. She played in an all-star tournament in Las Vegas the week before and got hurt on a water slide after the last game. She had stitches under one eye that *she* didn't feel should keep her from getting a chance to play against Jenny Circle, SHP's all-state center. Her parents disagreed, so she was forced to watch, to her great frustration.

My excitement lasted about 30 seconds, until Colleen informed me that she would be gone on vacation after Christmas. Aaahhhg! Natalie and Colleen gone. Karen still was not practicing with the team because of bad ankles. That makes three of my top players out.

Last Tuesday, the day before the SHP game, Jenny approached me before practice and said "I need to talk to you. You're not going to like this, but I'm not going to be able to make it to the game tomorrow." Aaaahhhhgg! It turned out that she was making college visits to see which school she would like to attend next year.

The situation was not pretty. I decided the day before the game that my personal goal for the game was to *not* tell Mike Ciardello, the SHP coach and one of the winningest high school coaches in the nation, that I was playing with four of my top players gone and relying on four junior-varsity players for significant playing time. I thought that would be a character-building goal for myself. It just seemed too easy to whine and I really didn't want to do that. I wanted to retain some small portion of dignity.

SHP made two quick baskets and then Haruka launched a three-pointer from the peanut gallery and swished it. I looked up at the scoreboard: SHP 4, Fremont 3. Not too bad, I thought. The next time I looked up it was SHP 30, Fremont 3. We ended up losing 78–18. I was proud of myself for two things. I was positive the entire game and I never once mentioned to the other coaches or the referees about our missing players. Nonetheless, we will *not* be in the Mitty tournament next year!

Kerry, up from the JV for the tournament, was happy. She told me the next day that this was the first time she had ever gotten her name in the paper for scoring points in a real game. So it wasn't a total fiasco!

Journal Entry—December 31, 1995

Yesterday in practice I think I turned things around. We were scrimmaging the JV team and playing horribly. I was so negative it was disgusting. Finally I remembered my own idea of positive charting (Positive charting is described on p. 39 of *Positive Coaching*). I stopped coaching (i.e. screaming) from the sidelines and began to chart the positive things I saw players doing. When we took a break I shared with the players who had done what positive things. The atmosphere turned around almost immediately. As soon as the players knew I was watching for positive things they began to block out, played tenacious defense, make second efforts for rebounds, etc. It was beautiful to behold. Why had I forgotten the power of postive charting for so long? It's like I've been in a fog for a month or more. I finally felt like the coach who wrote *Positive Coaching* rather than one who desperately needed to read it!

There is a saying in the twelve-step movement known as H-A-L-T. Don't let yourself get too Hungry-Angry-Lonely-or-Tired. Those emotions tend to break down our resolve to do what we know to be right. For alcoholics or overeaters, it means temptation to indulge in alcohol or food binging. For a coach, physical and emotional exhaustion can lead to throwing temper tantrums. I realize that the combination of my job, teaching Learning to Lead, coaching, and my parents' health problems have left me exhausted recently. While I don't know about hunger or loneliness, I certainly have experienced way too much anger this month. For the first time I can remember basketball has stopped being fun. Today I began to remember how beautiful and exciting this game is, regardless of who wins.

Journal Entry—January 3, 1996

Dark December *officially* ended yesterday. We beat Cupertino 50–46. My lifetime record at Cupertino High School is now 1–7! Afterwards, Colleen said to me "The players talked it over and we think you can shave now. And not any too soon either." I guess I could interpret that two ways. The positive is that they think my coaching has improved. Or it could just mean they think the beard is ugly. Maybe both. Doesn't matter. I'm glad to get a win and glad to be in January!

Chapter 5

Ta-Dah!
The Coach as Linguist

The finest eloquence is that which gets things done.
—David Lloyd George

Words have power, and coaches who fail to develop and define their own vocabulary are overlooking a valuable tool. A team that has its own meaning-laden phrases is like a club with a secret handshake. Most coaches, if we will admit it, have enough of the child in us that we get a thrill out of secret codes, and the players certainly enjoy it. But beyond the cuteness of it, a personalized team vocabulary can be a source of motivation and an effective team-building technique.

Coaches as Data Compressors

One way of looking at what slogans and a personalized team vocabulary do for a team is to think of it as the equivalent of data compression in high-speed data communication. It saves time, a lot of time. And when you are in the middle of a fiercely contested basketball game, quick, accurate communication can mean the difference between excellent performance and stumbling.

Nicholas Negroponte, founding director of the Media Lab at MIT, in his book *Being Digital* describes a situation in which he and his wife are at a dinner party:

> Imagine six animated people having dinner around a table; they are deeply engrossed in a common discussion about, say, a person not there. During one moment of this discourse about Mr. X, I look across the table at my wife and wink. After dinner, you come up to me and say "Nicholas, I saw you wink at Elaine. What did you tell her?"

It turns out Negroponte and his wife had had dinner with Mr. X two nights earlier and knew some of the gossip about him was incorrect.

> What is happening in this example is that the transmitter (me) and the receiver (Elaine) hold a common body of knowledge, and thus communication between us can be in shorthand. In this example, I fire a certain bit through the ether and it expands in her head, triggering much more information. When you ask me what I said, I am forced to deliver to you all 100,000 bits. I lose the 100,000-to-1 data compression.

I like the image of a coach and players sharing so much common experience and knowledge that individual bits (say, a word or phrase from the coach or one of the players) can be fired into the ether of the court and the receivers (the entire team) can expand that phrase into an understanding of what they need to do next without the delay or cost of taking a scarce timeout.

Creating a Team Vocabulary

I used to have a predilection against phrases that sports coaches used to fire their teams up. Partly that was because they often seem trite ("No pain, no gain"), partly because they seemed anti-intellectual in their surreal simplicity (a high school coach saying to me as I walked the hall with my girlfriend, "Are you a lover or a fighter, Thompson?"), partly because they just seemed too easy to parrot without a corresponding commitment ("Ya gotta be tough!").

But over the years I have come to view the creation of a team vocabulary as an important tool for the building of the team itself. And it helps when someone like Negroponte provides the rationale for it being a cool, high-tech kind of thing to do. If there is a common base of experience developed around a word or phrase, so that it has a special meaning to that particular team, it can be both a powerful reminder of why additional effort is needed *right now* (something that is easy to forget when one is already very, very tired), and a trigger to release that effort.

S = E/T

Perhaps one of the smartest things I did early on was to develop a handy formula for success: S = E/T. We put this on the back of our practice jerseys, on T-shirts, on communications to parents and players, just about everywhere.

S = E/T means "success comes from effort over time." While not completely idiot-proof (it is possible to make *futile* efforts over a long period of time), this is a formula of tremendous power. What it says is that you only have to keep on keeping on to be successful. To be successful in most aspects of life, what you really need most is staying power.

Yes, natural talent is important,* intelligence is important, a love of what you are doing is important. And those attributes are not things that are equitably distributed throughout our world.

But if you are willing to work hard, you will get better. And if you are willing to continue your effort over a long period of time, you will succeed. That is not to say you will be "the greatest." There can only be one "greatest" in any field. But success is less scarce in the world.

If you want to be an attorney, you don't need to be the greatest attorney in the world. You need to have some interest in and felicity for the law. And then you need to study hard and get some experience and learn from it and then, *if you keep it up*, you will be a successful attorney.

---

*In *Positive Coaching* I introduced the acronym D-I-M-I-T-T which stands for "determination is more important than talent." Like S = E/T, this is universally true. Talent is a gift, something you are born with. But determination is what you can bring to the table regardless of how lucky you happened to be at birth.

George Leonard defines mastery as "the path of patient, dedicated effort without attachment to immediate results." And patient, dedicated effort over time will lead to success. As someone once said, "Successful people do what unsuccessful people aren't willing to do."

Our formula of S = E/T helped reinforce a work ethic that helped us on the playing court and, I am convinced, will help the girls become successful at whatever they do the rest of their lives.

Strong and Beautiful

Another phrase that we used often was "strong and beautiful," usually with the emphasis on the "and." I wanted to convey to the players that strength was not an exclusively masculine characteristic. Women have been strong throughout history but usually haven't gotten credit for it because their strength has rarely been trumpeted on the battlefield. I also wanted to counter the idea that as women become physically (or psychologically!) stronger, they become less attractive to men. As a friend's t-shirt says, "Real men marry athletes."

Ultimately, I wanted to reconfigure the definition of *beauty* away from one based solely on physical looks to include the inner beauty that comes from strength of character. I wanted to encourage my players to consider the notion that external beauty (what society considers beautiful in a woman) is ultimately not as valuable as the more durable beauty that comes from having a strong character. I felt this was important because we cannot control how we look, except in very minor ways, but over time, each of us can have a lot of control over how much character we develop and thus over how much inner beauty shines through.*

Every day when I came to practice we needed to pull out a section of the bleachers so we could use the scoreboard and clock for our drills. This task required three people, so I asked for some volunteers to help me pull out the bleachers. Since this was not one of the girls' favorite tasks, I began to ask them by saying that I needed a couple of strong and beautiful players to help me.

---

*There is a story I once heard about Abraham Lincoln. Lincoln allegedly told Secretary of War Stanton to fire a general during the Civil War. Stanton asked him why and the President responded that he didn't like the man's face. Stanton protested that you couldn't fire someone because of the way he looked, something over which he had no control. To which Lincoln replied, "After the age of 40, everyone is responsible for his own face."

From that point on I used the strong-and-beautiful phrase often. I had been reading Madeleine Blais' book *In These Girls, Hope Is a Muscle* and was intrigued by one of the captains of the Amherst High School team having a "strong woman wall" in her bedroom on which she put pictures of women she admired.

Once I asked each girl to bring to practice a picture of a strong woman she admired. Over the next few practices, each player would show her picture and talk about the characteristics of that woman she admired. This was the first time I had ever heard of Gabrielle Reece, who doubles as a model and a top-level volleyball player. Several of the girls brought her picture, which was perfect since she is clearly both strong and beautiful in the conventional, external sense. She lifts weights, and one might even say she is more attractive because of her physical strength.

One player momentarily threw me for a loop by bringing in a picture of Deion Sanders, the professional football player, then playing for the San Francisco 49ers. I started to make some snide comment about her not being clear on the concept, but caught myself and held my tongue. I asked her why she had brought a picture of Sanders, someone I had not thought of as an obvious candidate for a role model even without the problem of being the wrong gender.

Her response made me glad I had buttoned my lip. She said that Sanders had never taken a drink of alcohol and had vowed that he never would. Whatever one might think of Deion Sanders, this is a characteristic that is admirable and we were able to have a good conversation about that with the entire team.

Nonetheless, I was not certain that the strong-and-beautiful message was getting through. Several of the girls seemed a little embarrassed to talk about their strong woman picture (although each did) and I wasn't sure whether that was because of the novelty of having that kind of a discussion during a basketball practice or if they just thought it was dumb.

It wasn't until after the season that I received some evidence that the phrase had taken. The girls presented me with a framed photo of the team dressed to kill in black evening gowns with their arms flexed like body builders. Haruka, the smallest player, was in the middle with both arms flexed and a particularly intense expression on her face. The silver frame was engraved with the magic words: "WWF: Strong and Beautiful."

I couldn't have asked for a more wonderful present. And when the returning players began lifting weights regularly in the off-season, I

knew that they truly understood that the two characteristics were reinforcing rather than mutually exclusive.

FOUR!

In November 1994 Jeff McKay and I decided to go to the Stanford-
Washington football game. We both were on the Stanford campus that
Saturday and agreed we'd see as much of the game as possible when we
finished our meetings. It was a rainy day and we got to the Stanford
Stadium just after half-time. Because the weather was so bad there were
lots of empty seats right on the fifty-yard line. We were dressed for bad
weather so we were ecstatic to have such good seats, even in the down-
pour.

We watched as Stanford protected a small lead throughout the third
quarter. As the gun sounded to end the third quarter, the Washington
players came running off the field holding up four fingers and waving
them at each other. We pondered this for a moment and then realized
that they were signaling to each other: "The fourth quarter belongs to us!"

The Husky players believed that if they were close to the other team
at the end of the third quarter, their superior conditioning and mental
toughness meant that they would win the game because they would dominate in the fourth quarter. As it turned out, they were wrong. Stanford
not only held the lead but extended it on some terrific running out of the
quarterback position by Scott Frost, the back-up who replaced the injured starter Steve Stenstrom.

I could barely wait until the next basketball practice. I told the girls
about my experience, much as I've related it here. I said that I wanted our
team to be in such good physical condition and so mentally tough that if
we were close to the other team at the start of the fourth quarter we would
be confident that we would win the game. We developed a cheer that we
began to use to break from the huddle in the fourth quarter.

We always broke from the huddle with a word such as "Defense!" or
"Rebound!" or "DIMITT!" Sometimes I would supply the word to prompt
them to focus on the part of the game that I felt most needed it. Often I
would ask one of the team leaders to supply the word. Whoever provided
the word would say "1-2-3" and then we all would shout out the word of
the huddle, as in "1-2-3-Defense!"

From this point on however, we always broke from huddles in the fourth quarter with a cheer of "1-2-3-FOUR!" to symbolize our confidence that we were in better shape and determined to be mentally tougher than the other team, and that we were going to win the game. We also stole Washington's signal—four fingers shown to each other to signify our determination to dominate in the fourth quarter. It usually happened that we *were* in better shape, and we won more than our share of close games in the fourth quarter.

Perhaps the most wonderful thing that happened after we began working with the idea of "FOUR!" occurred in practice. We would typically run wind sprints three times during a practice. Once was right after warm-ups to get people in the spirit of working hard. We would also usually end practice with some running. But perhaps the most grueling were the mid-practice sprints. These were tougher than the other two because at the beginning of practice the players were rested. At the end they knew that if they could just get through this little bit more, practice was over. But the wind sprints in the middle came at a time when players were already tired and knowing there was a lot more work to be done.

One day a few weeks after I introduced the "FOUR!" idea, we were running the mid-practice wind sprints. In between wind sprints 3 and 4 I looked down the row of wheezing, bent-over players to see Shauna flashing me four fingers. At that point I knew we were on to something.

Ta-Dah!

One metaphor for leadership we used in Learning to Lead was the "leader as improviser." The best plans in the world can be rendered obsolete by a shock in the external world. Leaders who are tied to a script are less likely to be successful than those who are able to improvise when other people and events deviate from the script. We wanted to encourage our students to develop more than one arrow for their leadership quiver, to not believe that their habitual mode of leading was the only way. And we wanted to convey the message that it isn't an either-or situation: effective improvisation doesn't mean lack of preparation.

We watched excerpts that Debra Meyerson had selected from *Hearts of Darkness*, a documentary film about the making of Francis Ford Coppola's film *Apocalypse Now*. In it there is a scene in which Coppola gently chides actor Dennis Hopper for not knowing his lines. Hopper, perplexed, says "But you told us to forget the lines." Coppola responds "To forget your lines you have to know them first." Ah . . .

Debra asked Patricia Ryan (from the Stanford drama department) to conduct a session on improvisation for the class that was a real eye-opener. Ryan's improvisation workshop contained many gems but my favorite was "Ta-dah!"

Ryan emphasized how important it was in becoming a good impro-viser, to allow oneself to make mistakes, and in fact to incorporate any mistakes into the improvisation. She asked if we had ever noticed what a circus clown does when he makes a mistake. Instead of shrinking up and berating himself silently with "Oh, no, I really screwed up!" he turns to the crowd on one side and takes a magnificent bow with his hands ex-tended and his wrists flung wide and says "Ta-dah!" as if he had just pulled off a master stunt. Then he turns to face the audience on the other side and repeats the bow, "Ta-dah!"

Ryan had a powerful personal story to illustrate her point. In 1992, when Gerhard Casper was inaugurated as Stanford University's President, Ryan was asked to participate in the program and read an ex-cerpt from Jane Stanford's diary. Patricia Ryan found herself on the dais with presidents of countries, supreme court justices, and other distin-guished personages. As she prepared herself for her performance, she took a last look at the program to make sure she knew when she was on. The program listed her right after the Stanford orchestra.

As the orchestra ended its piece, Ryan got up, walked to the podium, and spoke into the microphone "And now a word from Jane Stanford." At that moment the Stanford orchestra resumed playing. Ryan had mis-taken their pause between movements for the end of the piece. She was mortified as she walked back to her seat. In her head she repeated mantra-like "Ta-dah! Ta-dah! Ta-dah!"

When the orchestra finished (this time waiting until she was *sure* they were finished!), she again got up and walked to the podium and began again, "And now a word from Jane Stanford."

I shared this story with my players, as well as John Wooden's quote that the team that makes the most mistakes is going to win. I stressed that we want to be aggressive, the kind of team that made things happen, and if we played that kind of basketball, we would occasionally make a mistake. I encouraged them to say "Ta-dah!" to themselves whenever they screwed up. From then on, when someone would make a mistake in practice, they would turn toward me and shout "Ta-dah!" with their hands outstretched in the circus performer's bow as they ran down the court. I told the players that I would know they were really playing with abandon if one of them let out a Ta-dah! after making a mistake in a game. That never happened, but I was happy at least that Ta-dah! became a staple of practices.

Zero-Zero

One of the problems our team faced was a drop-off in intensity during the third quarter. We generally did well in the fourth quarter, thanks to "FOUR!" and our excellent conditioning. But we often seemed to go to sleep in the third quarter, giving up leads that we had taken into the locker room at half-time, occasionally falling so far behind that we had no chance of catching up in the fourth quarter regardless of how well we played.

I tried to think of ways of maintaining our intensity during the third quarter and finally hit on the idea that we needed to begin the third quarter as if we were playing an entirely new game. I introduced this idea in the half-time locker room of a game in which we held a comfortable lead. "We need to play the third quarter as if the score is zero-zero." I emphasized this several times in the next few minutes, not yet realizing that I was on to something more lasting.

We went out and built on our lead, winning handily. By the next game I had forgotten about zero-zero. I also had forgotten to check the scoreboard as I left the floor to come to the locker room, so I asked Leticia, my assistant coach, "What's the score?" Before she could answer, Chi shouted out "Zero-zero!" I had to laugh and admit that she was right. And, I'm happy to report, our intensity level in the third quarter did stay at a high level, which was perhaps yet another reason why The Streak happened.

Five or Twelve?

There are also times when a phrase can be helpful for an individual who is working on a specific aspect of her game. Chi, a sophomore with tremendous potential, was quick, had a good outside shot, and played terrific defense. Her biggest problem was that she seemed to lose concentration on drives to the basket just before she shot. She would make a brilliant move to the basket and then heave it up rather than focusing on the rim and taking a shot that had a chance of going in.

Early in her sophomore year, by which time she had earned a starting position, I told her that she would certainly score five points a game no matter what. Her natural ability would get her some steals and easy lay-ups so she would get her five points. She had the potential to average 12 points a game if she were able to really focus on the delivery of the shot and not simply toss it up.

From that point on whenever she would toss up a *hoper* (as in "I hope it goes in"), I would yell out "Five or twelve?" Sometimes I might add "You get to decide." Sure enough, as the season progressed she began to increase the intensity and duration of her concentration as she took her shots off the drive. I remember a key moment in a crucial game during The Streak when she stole the ball at mid-court and drove to the basket under heavy pressure from two opposing players. Chi had about a step on them but they were gaining fast as she got to the basket. Her concentration as she put the ball up on the glass was exquisite. You could almost feel how hard she was focusing on the basket and ignoring the opposing players. When the ball dropped through the net, the entire team went crazy, not only because the basket helped seal a close win, but because everyone could see a tangible symbol of Chi's transformation right in front of them.

Redefining Winning: The Ultimate Linguistic Challenge

If S = E/T helped us redefine *success,* the other word that I felt needed to be redefined was "winner." In this society, all too often first place is the only definition of winning. Two of the maxims I hate most are "Second place is no place" and "Another word for second place—Loser."

One of the most inspirational leadership stories of our time (and all time!) is that of Mahatma Gandhi's leading the people of the Indian subcontinent to freedom from the British. In *Gandhi: The Traditional Roots of Charisma,* Suzanne and Lloyd Rudolph attribute a large part of Gandhi's success in arousing heroic mass action in a people demoralized by British colonialism to his ability to redefine the meaning of courage.

"The prevailing Western definitions of courage . . . have generally stressed masterly aggressiveness, taking as their model the soldier willing and eager to charge with fixed bayonet the numerically superior enemy in a heroic act of self-assertion."

Gandhi realized physical revolt against the military might of the British was self-defeating. But, rather than accepting the British view of Indians as weak and cowardly—a definition that all too many Indians themselves had bought into—he redefined the entire notion of courage. Again, the Rudolphs: "Gandhi turned the moral tables on the English definition of courage by suggesting that aggression was the path to mastery of those *without* self-control, non-violent resistance the path of those *with* control (emphasis added)." Non-violent resistance became the signature tool by which individual Indians demonstrated their courage and gained psychological liberation, which in turn led to political independence for the Indian subcontinent.

Over the years of coaching, I have often shown my players an excerpt from the movie *Gandhi* in which Gandhi is repeatedly knocked down during a protest. Time after time he gets back up. I emphasize with my players (usually after a difficult loss) that being a winner means getting back up. Over time you will prevail if you keep getting back up.

In January 1995 we lost a close game to Lynbrook High School when we missed a lot of "easy" shots (easy, that is, to those of us on the sidelines who didn't have to make them!).

Haruka took five three-pointers and missed all of them, although three of them rimmed in and out. Late in the game we were down by five with just over a minute to go. We had the ball and needed a three to get us back into it. Haruka found herself open beyond the three-point line. She looked at the basket, gave a brief shake of the head, and then passed to Jenny. Jenny knew we needed a three so she passed it back to Haruka. Haruka was still open but again she passed the ball. I called timeout.

In the huddle I told Haruka that we needed a three and that she should shoot if she got open. She had her head down but she nodded in seeming understanding. When play resumed, Haruka again found herself open beyond the three-point line and again passed rather than take the shot.

After the game I asked Haruka why she hadn't shot. She then told me what there hadn't been time to explain in the huddle during our brief timeout. She felt that she had let the team down by missing her first five shots and she didn't want to let them down again by missing another shot. I now understood why she had her head down in the huddle. Her nodding her head didn't mean "I understand what you are saying and I will go out there and do it!" It simply meant "You are my coach and I respect you." This was not the first time I realized that there were cultural differences between Japanese and American youth, but I had never experienced it in such a dramatic fashion.

I stressed to Haruka that the team needed her to shoot threes, that if she missed twenty in a row, I still wanted her to shoot the twenty-first time if she was open, that she was not letting us down when she missed. She nodded her head, this time in complete agreement rather than simply acknowledging that she had heard me.

The next day I arrived at the gym just before practice to find Haruka on the floor shooting threes. By the amount of sweat running down her face, I could tell that she had been there for some time.

Our next game, Haruka made three of four three-pointers, hit another two-pointer with one foot on the three-point line, and then sank four consecutive free throws late in the game to seal the victory against a team that had beaten us earlier in the season.

In the locker room after the game I told the team that we had seen a perfect example of a "winner" in action in Haruka that night. I reminded them of what had happened during the Lynbrook game and the entire team cheered Haruka. But I wanted to make sure they understood exactly what I meant by "winner." I told them that it was really nice that Haruka had made those shots, but the point at which she demonstrated that she was a winner was when she came into practice early to work on her shooting. It is the getting-back-up that makes one a winner, not whether one then goes on to make the key shots. I really was happy that she had made those key shots and that we had won the game, but in a larger sense it didn't really matter. Haruka was a winner, make or miss.

Take-Aways

The Coach as Linguist

1. Recognize the power that a team vocabulary can have to build the team.

2. Develop the key characteristics or values you want your team to personify and write them down.
   a. Create or "steal" phrases that communicate each characteristic.
   b. Look for stories from the larger world of sports and life that illustrate the characteristic and share them often with the players.
   c. Look for and call the team's attention to examples of situations when your own players exemplify those characteristics.
   d. Emblazon the phrases on team t-shirts, practice jerseys, correspondence to parents, locker room signs, etc., to encourage players to internalize them.

3. Identify the current phrases your team uses that have meanings not obvious to outsiders. If any of them undermine the values you identified, develop a plan to eradicate them.

4. Redefine terms that have general meaning. "Success" and "winner" can have a specific meaning to your team that encourages effort and perseverance.
   a. Ask players to bring pictures of people who exemplify some characteristic that they want to attain.
   b. Ask players to share with the team why they admire this person.

5. Involve players in suggesting and defining terms for the team vocabulary.

Chapter 6

Shooting in the Dark:
The Entwining of Effort and Enjoyment

Are we dancing our life? It is all a matter of awareness. The more deeply we see into life, the more clearly we perceive the dance. Pursuing reality down into the heart of the atom, we find nothing at all except vibration, music, dancing. And the world of our senses is also dancing. (Spider web shimmering in the sunrise, trees sweeping the wind, cars burning along the highway, blood pulsing behind our eyes.) We only have to become aware, and we find ourselves dancing too. . . We have won the game. But how did we feel from the inside while we were doing it? Did we dance?

—George Leonard, **The Ultimate Athlete**

For many years my wife has been adamant about working out on a regular basis. For her, mornings are like clockwork—she pops out of bed, dons her running gear, and is onto the street in the time it takes me to roll over. For most of my life I have avoided running as boring and tedious, preferring competitive sports such as basketball or tennis as ways to stay in shape. In recent years, however, I have come to value running almost as much for what it does for my mental state as for my physical conditioning. Whenever I am troubled by something, I invariably feel better able to deal with it after a run. In addition to serving as an anti-depressant, exercise often presents a bonus as ideas on how to approach a given problem come to me while I run.

Recently, my mother called to tell me about the cardiac rehabilitation exercise program that was part of her recovery from her bypass operation. She spoke excitedly for some time about her workout routine, ending with "I've never understood how you and Sandy could enjoy exercising as much as you seem to, until now." The next day I remembered her words as I was finishing a session on the treadmill. Sweat was pouring down my face and life was just terrific. I realized that enjoyment is exactly the right word for what I felt in that moment. I love the feeling of a shirt that is dripping wet with sweat. Although there is discomfort involved in working out, the prevailing nature of the experience is pleasure. And the source of the pleasure is the effort itself.

When Effort and Enjoyment Merge

As a coach, I will feel successful, regardless of my team's record, if I can get my players to make huge efforts. And I will be happy beyond words if I can help them to enjoy the process of making huge efforts.

There are a handful of times in my life when effort and enjoyment merged and there was really no distinction in my experience between the two. Among them:

- At Macalester College in the late 1960s, John Simpson and I developed a proposal to create Inner College, an experimental college within Macalester. We assembled a group of dissident students and successfully lobbied the administration and faculty to make it happen. The intense effort required to develop the proposal and sell it to the faculty was excruciatingly fun. I now look back on the experience of hard work during the year leading up to the experimental college as more enjoyable than the year of the experiment itself.

- I remember waking up from a Sunday afternoon nap on the couch in our apartment in Rock Springs, Wyoming, in 1975. I was sweating like a stuck pig from a terrifying dream in which I forgot my lines during a performance. I had played the part of Charlie Dalrymple in a classroom teachers association production of *Brigadoon*, the final performance had been the night before, and I was suffering from performance withdrawal. After I calmed myself, I realized that in addition to being relieved that this huge commitment was fulfilled, I was sad that it was over.

- In 1981, at the Oregon Department of Energy, I was part of an effort to develop a state energy conservation strategy for Governor

Vic Atiyeh. Putting together a comprehensive energy conservation program in a matter of months on which a conservative Republican governor and a liberal Democratic legislature could agree was a colossal amount of work. I remember one night at the end of one in a series of 14-hour days, Larry Gray and I were moaning about how hard we were working when Bill Sanderson, the most experienced political operative in the department, came by and overheard our complaining. He quieted us with "Quit your complaining. Most state employees spend their days dropping bricks down a well waiting to hear the splash." He was reminding us what a privilege it was to have the Governor and the Legislature waiting to see what we were going to come up with, and we took it to heart, drastically reduced our whining, and began to enjoy the experience.

Often, as above, it isn't clear to participants how much they enjoy making the effort until the experience is over. Mihaly Csikszentmihalyi, in his book *Flow: The Psychology of Optimal Experience*, notes how our feelings about an experience can mature over time: "Closing a contested business deal, or any piece of work well done, is enjoyable. None of these experiences may be particularly pleasurable at the time they are taking place, but afterward we think back on them and say 'That was really fun' and wish they would happen again."

There is a moving scene in an outstanding television series called *Against the Grain* that appeared all too briefly during the fall of 1993. The hero is an insurance agent who was a star quarterback in high school. His car is hit by a truck and he spends several months in the hospital recuperating. While recovering, he realizes he isn't happy with his line of work, that he wants to work with kids, that he wants to be a football coach. In the final scene of the premier episode, he is in the locker room talking to his team just before they take the field for their first game of the season. After giving them an inspirational message, he pauses and says "This is what it's all about, boys. I just wish I were 20 years younger." After a long pause, he says "Go on out there and have fun!"

Dick DeVenzio put it this way: "Athletes go through school playing mere games and preparing for life, for becoming doctors and lawyers and so forth. And doctors and lawyers wait for five o'clock so they can leave work, maybe catch the game of the week on TV, and sit around and talk of the good old days—when they were young athletes." Annie van den Toorn, my assistant coach during the 1995–96 season, regularly reminded the girls that the experience of playing high school basketball was something very special, something they would look back on their entire life. She had loved her all-state high school basketball career in Novato, California, and she encouraged them to value their high school experience even while they were running liners.

I wanted my players to realize the specialness of this experience, *while* they were going through it, not twenty years later. I wanted to help my players come early to the insight that took me decades to learn—that effort and enjoyment aren't incompatible. In fact, that they can merge and converge in intriguing and joyful ways. Making great efforts can become almost addictive.

How exactly does a coach get players to make big efforts? I decided to ask an expert, a coach who is reknowned for her ability to get players to work hard. I asked Tara VanDerveer, who had just been appointed coach of the U.S. Olympic womens' basketball team, to speak to our Learning to Lead students about her view of leadership. As she always does, she gave a high-intensity, insight-filled talk.

But afterwards, as we were talking outside the classroom, I realized I still didn't understand how she gets her players to work so hard. So I asked her "What specifically do you *do* to get your players to work so hard?" She shared two insights with me.

The Hardest Worker (Part One)

VanDerveer's first response: "The best player on the team has to be the hardest worker." When I think about players who work hard, I tend to remember guys from my high school days who didn't have a great deal of talent but compensated by diving for balls, hustling back on defense, and generally giving the proverbial 110% effort at every drill. That was fine for the lesser talents, but that kind of effort seemed almost unseemly for the best players on the team.

This isn't only the case in sports. I remember a conversation I had with the Director of the Oregon Department of Commerce years ago. Perhaps because I was a young whippersnapper, she gave me some professional advice about status in business meetings. She said that lower-status people come to meetings with bulging briefcases, thick notebooks, and manilla file folders, and they take lots of notes. Middle-level managers may have a simple pad of paper or a small pocket note-book that they use only sparingly. The highest-status people, often accompanied by the staff with the bulging briefcases, carry only an en-velope (presumably a letter they just received). And perhaps once (twice if the meeting is especially long) they will jot just a few words on the back of the envelope, and then only when something truly brilliant has been said.

Now in basketball this is virtually a rule: talent has its privileges. As a Chicago Bulls fan, I am irate every time Patrick Ewing takes his four-step move to the basket, unencumbered by the need to dribble, undis-tracted by the referee's whistle. Meanwhile, poor Luc Longley gets a foul for so much as daring to stretch his hands up in Ewing's face when he's about to shoot. Over and over again I read about NBA superstars getting preferential treatment, and the thing that irks me more than anything is that the lesser players, the fans, and even the referees seem to think "He's a superstar so he's earned it." (I have to admit, it doesn't seem to bother me quite as much when Michael Jordan or Scottie Pippen take just the slightest extra little inconsequential step on their way to the basket!)

One of the privileges of talent has always been that you didn't have to work so hard because you could accomplish more than the lesser lights without the indignity of having to try so hard. Coaches tend to feed into this because they (we!) recognize talent and appreciate what it can do for us. We tend to overlook it when the star loafs during condi-tioning drills because we depend on the star for our success. But Tara had turned this upside down: with talent comes responsibility! If you want to run with the big dogs, you need to get your lead dog(s) to set the pace. The stars have to work harder than the subs!

During the 1996 NBA playoffs, Bob Costas interviewed four substi-tutes for the Chicago Bulls: Steve Kerr, Bill Wennington, Judd Buechler, and Randy Brown. Costas asked them what they had learned from prac-ticing every day against Michael Jordan, Scottie Pippen, and Dennis Rodman. Wennington answered much as Tara VanDerveer had done: "How hard they work. They come out every day and give it 100%, and if you don't match them, they make you pay and you hear about it."

There are many reasons why the Chicago Bulls won the NBA Championship in 1996—great coaching, three of the best players to play the game, the league's Sixth Man of the year, and role players who were happy to contribute without complaining about wanting more playing time. But certainly a major part of why the Bulls won an NBA record number of victories was that their best players refused to rest on their talent and set a standard of hard work for the entire team.

I thought about who our hardest workers were and it wasn't obvious that it was the best players. I soon had the opportunity to raise this issue with Jenny and Colleen, who had accounted for more than half of our points last season and were the team leaders in assists and rebounds, respectively. It wasn't that they didn't work hard, because they did. It's just that they were quiet about it and I wanted them to be more obvious and vocal about setting a standard for hard work.

Journal Entry — November 12, 1995

How do I get myself into these things?! Friday was a vacation day for Fremont and a lot of the players had plans for the day. They wanted to practice in the morning so they'd have the rest of the day free. My only problem was that Learning to Lead meets at 8:00 A.M. on Fridays. I jokingly told them that I would be willing to practice in the morning if we went from 5:30 to 7:30 so I could make it to my eight o'clock class. Shauna immediately said, "I can do that." Not realizing the thin ice I was on, I said "Yeah, well maybe you're willing to get up that early, but I don't think everyone else is." Colleen and Jenny said in unison "I will." Pretty soon everyone had agreed to it. So, we began practice in the dark the next morning in a very cold gym at 5:30. It actually was a pretty good practice and I think everyone felt proud of being willing to make a voluntary sacrifice for the team.

The Hardest Worker (Part Two)

The second insight I got from VanDerveer is that the *coach* has to be the hardest worker: "I tell my players that they will not outwork me." I asked her if this challenge engenders some competition between the players and herself and she said that it did. Healthy competition.

This resonated with me immediately. When I first became Director of the Stanford Business School's Public Management Program, I threw myself into the program with tremendous zeal. I was so thrilled to have the job that I didn't even think of it as work (I still don't, actually). At the end of my first year, which had exceeded the expectations of everyone involved, including me, I had an insightful conversation with John King, one of the student leaders of the PMP. He said that part of the reason things had gone so well that year was because all the students saw how hard I was working to make the program better, and it was contagious.

As a coach I spent hundreds of dollars on coaching videotapes and books. I borrowed other tapes and books from friends who also were coaches. I reviewed and re-reviewed tapes until I understood and could teach my players the intricacies of a pressure defense or a zone offense or a last second out-of-bounds play. I picked the brains of coaches and former professional and college athletes about what to do in individual situations. I regularly woke up at 3 A.M. with ideas and began diagramming plays. I spent nearly as much time planning practices as it took to run them. I was constantly thinking about how to help my team get better. After my conversation with Tara, I realized that I needed to let my players know about my efforts. This was hard for me because I was raised in a time and place (North Dakota a long time ago!) in which you just didn't toot your own horn. But Tara helped me realize that much of the effort a coach makes is invisible to the players, and there is no substitute for letting the players know that their substantial commitment is matched by the coach.

I began to tell my players about the time I was spending watching coaching videotapes and reading basketball books. I wanted them to know, for example, that the reason we were able to implement a new defensive set was because I had spent the considerable time necessary to learn it so I could teach it to them. If I wanted Jenny and Colleen to make their efforts more visible, then I needed to make mine more visible.

Alignment and a Sense of Possibility

There is another factor in promoting an ethic of hard work that has to do with a group's sense of possibility for itself. Individual efforts aren't enough if there is a sense that the team isn't going anywhere. Peter Senge notes in *The Fifth Discipline* the importance to a successful team of the phenomenon of alignment, "when a group of people function as a whole."

> The fundamental characteristic of the relatively unaligned team is wasted energy. Individuals may work extraordinarily hard, but their efforts do not efficiently translate to team effort. By contrast, when a team becomes more aligned, a commonality of direction emerges, and individuals' energies harmonize. There is less wasted energy. In fact, a resonance or synergy develops, like the "coherent" light of a laser rather than the incoherent and scattered light of a light bulb. There is commonality of purpose, a shared vision, and an understanding of how to complement one another's efforts. Individuals do not sacrifice their personal interests to the larger team vision; rather the shared vision becomes an extension of their personal visions.

When alignment isn't present, individual efforts begin to seem foolish. Hard work by an individual can result in deep frustration if the team is not aligned and going nowhere.

To create alignment with my team, I wanted to activate a sense of possibility about what they could accomplish. Back a few years, when NHL professional hockey first came to Northern California, a student of mine interviewed Kevin Constantine, the new head coach of the San Jose Sharks. Constantine shared with her the first words out of his mouth when he addressed the team for the first time after being named head coach: "Stanley Cup." He wanted to get his players excited about their collective possibility. He wanted to signal to his team that he had high expectations for them, and it worked like gangbusters . . . for a while. The Sharks surprised almost every external observer by going to the Stanley Cup playoffs in their third year, where they defeated the mighty Detroit Red Wings in the first round. Then, in the second round, they took the Toronto Maple Leafs to seven games before losing. Things didn't work out so well for Constantine after that, but for a couple of glorious seasons he had his team playing way over its collective head.

There is something tremendously exciting about being part of something bigger than yourself, especially if it is about making this a better world. There was a time in the late 1960s when, as a young college student, I felt a part of a movement of people working together to improve the country. It was a terrific feeling, way out of proportion to any actual

good I was doing. Tom Hayden, later to become a California state senator, was a founder of the Students for a Democratic Society (SDS) in the
late 1950s and early 1960s. His memoir of that time, *Reunion*, ends with
his statement of his feeling about being part of a movement for social
change: "Whatever the future holds, and as satisfying as my life is today,
I miss the sixties and always will."

When I was a Stanford MBA student from 1984 to 1986, Apple
Computer was *the* hot company to work for. When Apple recruiters came
to the GSB, they didn't talk about market share or making money, as
most companies did. They talked in mystical, reverent tones about
changing the world by putting user-friendly computers into every home
and office. Later, when I went to work for Hewlett Packard, HP employees talked longingly about the glory days of introducing and promoting
the initial HP LaserJet printer. Like the Macintosh, the LaserJet was a
product that changed the world of work by virtue of its small size and
low price. Laser printers began appearing *everywhere*, where before
LaserJet they had been limited to centralized typing pools and computer
centers.

However, I was involved with marketing a "mature" version of
LaserJet while getting ready for the introduction of the LaserJet II.
LaserJet was HP's biggest revenue-producing product and if there was a
hitch in the introduction of LaserJet II, the company could end up losing millions, perhaps billions, of dollars. However, while these activities
were of the utmost importance to the company, there was no longer the
transcendent sense that we were creating a product that could change
the world. Now the challenge was to market a product with slightly better features so as to justify a higher price than the copycat competitors
who had swarmed into the laser printer market since the success of the
original LaserJet. This didn't inspire the kind of mission-driven commitment experienced by the people who worked on the Macintosh and
the original LaserJet.

With the Women Warriors I hoped we could develop a shared sense
of possibility that would include such things as becoming our league's
champion, and making the CCS playoffs for only the second time in the
history of the school. I wanted them to feel that they were part of something bigger and more important than simply playing basketball for
themselves. I wanted them to begin to sense their possibility, so that
their hard work would be both a badge of honor and fun.

Effort and Friendship

Another important thing needs to be said about effort: it is often intimately tied to the development of friendship.

I once attended a panel discussion of Stanford Business School alumni who had started businesses. One fellow said he had started an adventure travel company with some people he liked and wanted to work with so he could become better friends with them. Many in the audience laughed at that and criticized it afterwards for being naive—after all, they said, you want to start a company with people who bring needed expertise to the table. But I think he was on to something.

I met many of my long-time friends through joint efforts of some kind. The college friends I am most in touch with are all fellow members and co-conspirators in the successful attempt to create Inner College within Macalester College. Chris Coleman and I forged a lifelong friendship as we struggled to help each other survive the MBA "core" during our first year of business school. The central relationship of my life, my partnership with my wife, was launched when Sandra and I worked together at the Behavioral Learning Center in St. Paul, Minnesota.

There is something purifying about making great efforts together that goes beyond the conventional meaning of *fun* and is not fully captured even in the more complex term, "enjoyment." Perhaps *meaning* is what I am talking about. John Gardner has said meaning is not something one stumbles across in life. We build meaning into our lives by the commitments we make. Lasting friendships are often forged in the crucible of shared commitment and struggle.

Journal Entry—December 12, 1995

Wednesday, something amazing happened. [GSB economics professor] John Roberts told me recently about a little-known justification for granting tenure to university faculty. He said that older faculty tend to be intimidated and even fearful of young faculty, whose new ideas may leave them behind. Tenure assures older faculty that they won't be replaced by brilliant young professors coming into the pipeline, even if the newer faculty are smarter. Since they don't have to worry about job security, the older faculty will be more likely to welcome rather than undercut, or even bar admission to, younger faculty. In that way, the academy will continually renew and improve itself with smarter and smarter people.

During Wednesday's practice we were having a shooting contest and Chi was talking trash to Shauna, who was on the other team. She told Shauna her team was going to beat Shauna's and went on about how much she would enjoy watching Shauna do the push-ups that were the mandatory consequences for the losers. I told Chi that I would pay more attention to her boasting if she were ever able to beat Shauna in a liner drill. Shauna is by no means the fastest player, but she is in such great shape and works so hard that she wins almost all the time. Chi is faster than Shauna but had never beaten her.

Shortly after that we did another set of liners. And wonder of wonders, Chi won it! I was a little uneasy, wondering how Shauna, senior co-captain, was going to take being beaten by upstart sophomore Chi. I shouldn't have worried. Shauna went right over to Chi and gave her a high five while the rest of the team clapped for Chi. Once again, I am amazed at Shauna's maturity and leadership.

Yesterday, Shauna won all the liners again.

Coaching to Peak

Tied to the sense of possibility is the belief that you are progressing. The feeling that you are improving can make huge efforts seem like fun. I first experienced this when I was a teacher aide at the Behavioral Learning Center in St. Paul, Minnesota, in the early 1970s. Under the leadership of a psychologist named Dick LaLiberte, we began charting the learning and behavioral progress of our "emotionally disturbed" and often "learning-disabled" children. It seemed to have a dramatic effect. The fact that they could *see* their progress made them work harder so they could see even *more* progress.

In our darkest days, I believe what held us together as a team, and what kept us working so hard, was our belief that we were learning and getting better. The way we characterized it was that we wanted to be playing our best basketball at playoff time. We wanted to peak at the end.

The history of sports is filled with examples of teams that get out of the gate ahead of the pack, only to peak in mid-season and then taper off just at the time when it is vital to be playing at the top of one's game. Teams start off like a ball of fire but seem to run out of gas by the time the playoffs come around. Other teams will start slow and build to a boil at just the right time. It's a bit of a mystery why some peak and others taper, but some recent social-science research on crime prevention gave me a new way of thinking about it.

An article in the June 3, 1996, *The New Yorker* by Malcolm Gladwell called "The Tipping Point" addressed the puzzle of why crime had decreased so dramatically and suddenly in New York City. People often refer to crime as a metaphorical "epidemic," but new social-science research is beginning to take seriously the notion that crime acts like a disease epidemic. Early in a crime wave (before it reaches epidemic proportions) a small increase in the number of crimes in an area may go unnoticed. If the increase continues, the "tipping point" may be reached and a precipitous increase occurs. What has been incremental and barely noticeable suddenly sweeps like a tidal wave over a geographic area.

As a crime-fighting policymaker, you would want to be aware of the existence of a reverse tipping point because until you reach it all of your efforts may seem to be much ado about nothing. Periodically, you could increase funding for anti-crime programs, institute community-based policy, put more cops on the street, etc., without much to show for it. But if you keep at it, assuming you're doing the right kinds of things, when you finally reach the tipping point things get better in a big hurry. When the tipping point is reached, the sudden and dramatic improvement seems out of proportion to the recent, incremental effort expended.

T.J. Rodgers, the CEO of Cypress Semiconductor, approached the same idea from a different angle when he addressed the Learning to Lead class. He drew points on the board that represented the various milestones a new product needs to meet for it to reach its revenue potential over its lifecycle.

After discussing each of the early milestones, he drew a line between the points connecting them into a graph. The area under the curve was the total amount of the potential revenue stream for the product over its lifecycle. He then overlaid another curve on the graph with a much smaller area beneath it. This was the amount of product revenue if the early milestones were not met, in some cases if they slipped by just a matter of a few weeks.

Because the chip industry is so competitive, small delays can mean that a competitor's product that gets to market more quickly can leave slim pickings for later entries. The stark difference in area between the two curves amounted to some real money.*

Just as small delays in the early development of a product have huge financial ramifications over the product's life cycle, a team that isn't progressing in the early stages of a season will not be able magically to jump to a higher level, regardless of how hard they work once the season begins. But the concept of the tipping point may help explain why a heretofore undistinguished team can reach a post-season tournament, for example, and seem to explode to a much higher level of performance, surprising observers and opponents alike. While the milestones that a chip maker is meeting (or not meeting) determine the ultimate potential of the product, they are not visible to the outside observer. Similarly, a team with a tarnished early-season record, but which is meeting important milestones not apparent to outside observers, can be poised to leapfrog teams that gave it great difficulty earlier in the season.

Of course, simply meeting early milestones doesn't guarantee ultimate success. A competitor may introduce a better chip at a lower price. Another team may improve as much or more than yours. And luck always can play an unanticipated role. But it's pretty much certain that you won't be in a position to reach the tipping point if you aren't making effective efforts and meeting important early milestones. If I want to meet my goal of running 1,100 miles in 1997, I need to knock off miles in January, February, and March. If I need to run ten miles on the last day of the year to make my goal, I may be able to do that. But I can't rely on being able to run ten miles every day in December to make up for missing earlier milestones.

I was fortunate twice to have a team peak at the end of the season. At the end of the 1996 season another coach asked me how we did it. In thinking how to respond I came up with my five-point prescription for why we peaked at the end.

1. *Make peaking a goal.* We talked about wanting to peak at the end and set it as a goal. We said again and again that we wanted to be

---

*I'm reminded of former U.S. Senate Minority Leader Everett Dirksen's famous statement about the Federal Budget: "A billion here and a billion there. Pretty soon, you're talking real money."

playing our best basketball at the end of the year. When we got hammered by some very good teams early in the pre-season, we used our peaking goal to help us learn from the defeats without getting discouraged. We were not yet all that we would be. By explicitly making peaking at the end a goal, we were partially inoculated against the poisonous psychological efects that early, and inevitable, setbacks can have—as long as we could see that we were improving.

2. *Schedule character-building games early.* My second year, when I had control of the scheduling (the schedule for my first year had been set before I was hired) I tried to schedule early the toughest non-conference teams I could find that wouldn't totally destroy and demoralize us. Then, when we lost to a strong team, we reminded ourselves that we had chosen a stronger schedule over a glittery record because we wanted to peak at the end. While this helped us toughen up, there is a down side to this approach. In both years I coached we received a lower seed in the playoffs than I thought we deserved, perhaps because the seeding committee gave more credence to our mediocre overall record than our sterling end-of-the-season record.

3. *Design practices for peaking.* A big part of the reason we were able to peak was that we didn't get tired of practicing as the season wore on. In fact, the players enjoyed practice. I often thought that the players' tears (and my own!) at the end of each of our seasons were as much about no longer being able to share practice together as about the pain of losing the game. We tried a lot of things to make practices fun and meaningful (see Chapter 4) and our conditioning increased as the year progressed, while some teams we played seemed to tire more easily toward the end of the year. It was as if they knew their season was going nowhere and they were just going through the motions until it was over. Our habits got better as the year progressed because so much of what we practiced was intended to reinforce them, which paid off the further into the season we got.

4. *Monitor improvement.* Mike Dunlap made several suggestions that were helpful to monitor how we were progressing during the

course of the season. One was to begin each practice with a full-court, figure-eight drill using a heavy ball. The heavy ball reinforced our passing and catching ability. Unlike boys, who generally have been playing with balls since they could toddle, many girls haven't developed the hand and wrist strength needed to catch and throw hard passes. Our agreement with each other was that we wouldn't move on to the rest of practice until we had made eight lay-ups in a row without the ball ever touching the floor. If a player had to dribble the ball to keep from travelling, we started the count over. If the ball hit the floor as it came through the net, we started over. During the course of the season we kept track of how long it took us to reach our number of consecutive baskets and when it became too easy to quickly reach our target, we increased the number to make it more challenging. Starting practice this way forced everyone to get into a state of high concentration right away. And, when we completed the exercise quickly, it gave us a visible reminder from practice to practice of how well we were progressing toward our goal of peaking at the end. When we were having a down day and it took us a long time to get to our goal, it was also useful as a wake-up call to increase the concentration and intensity.

5. *Expect to peak*. Finally, I think that we peaked because we believed we were going to peak. I tried to talk as confidently as I could with the players—even during the dark month of December 1995, when we lost every game—about how we were on track. Fortunately, the players themselves reinforced that message in their remarks after games and practices whenever we took stock of where we were and where we were headed.

Once the players returning for my second season had experienced peaking at the end despite a rocky beginning, they were confident it would happen again the next year. And it did.

Journal Entry—July 20, 1995

Yesterday when we got to Fremont for our Monday-Wednesday-Friday 7 A.M. workouts, the power was out in the small gym. We all stood around wondering what to do. I decided to find a janitor to see what needed to be done. I figured since no one besides the girls' basketball team was using the gym these days, maybe no one knew the power was out.

It took me about 20 minutes before I found Bob Stahl, the head custodian. He threw up his hands. The heavy rains over the weekend had knocked out the power in the entire school, and he and his staff had been working overtime trying to resolve the problem. The bottom line was that there would be no lights in the gym today.

When I got back, I thought everyone had gone home because everyone had disappeared. Then I noticed the gym door propped open. The players were in the gym shooting baskets! It was really black in there with just a bit of faint light coming through the doors at the four corners of the gym. It was almost as if they were shooting blind. It's inspiring for a coach to see players who love basketball and want to improve so much that they are willing to shoot in the dark. It would have been very easy for them to go home. They had a ready excuse, but they chose not to take it. I took some photos. I hope at least one turns out. I would love to make a big poster of them shooting in the dark to put up in the locker room next season with a caption something like "The team that loves basketball so much they even shoot in the dark."

Driving home I experimented with some new words to the tune of *Strangers in the Night*:

> Shooters in the dark
> Flinging three-pointers
> Wondering in the dark
> Did that one feel right?
> Did I hear a swish?
> Was that a perfect shot?
>
> Shooters in the dark
> We can't stop shooting
> Even in the dark
> We have a vision
> What we want to be
> We shooters in the dark.

Pedestrian lyrics perhaps, but an image to brighten any coach's heart!

Take-Aways

Effort and Enjoyment

1. Take your top player(s) aside and share with them the secret to getting an entire team to work incredibly hard—that their behavior sets the tone for how hard everyone else will work. Ask them to become the hardest workers and to become vocal and visible about it.

2. Share with your players your commitment to become the best coach you can be. Tell them you are going to work as hard at improving as a coach as they will at becoming better players. Make your efforts as a coach more visible to them by sharing with them the steps you are taking to become a better coach.

3. Share with your players your own joy in past efforts. Let them know how much you have enjoyed working hard in the past and that you want them to be able to enjoy the experience *right now* rather than only in retrospect. Ask them to tell you what they enjoy about the efforts they are making as part of this team.

4. Teach your players about the concept of alignment, in which everyone is pulling in the same direction, and how it is necessary if each individual's efforts are going to be productive. Ask them to suggest ways to improve the team's alignment. Continue to tie effort to the sense of possibility you see for the team and the goals you have set together.

5. Be aware that the people you are working with *right now*, even if you've just met them, may become treasured friends in the years to come. And your working together with them may be the source of those great friendships.

6. Develop a plan to help ensure that your team peaks at the most opportune time. Discuss with your players the importance of peaking and your thoughts about the milestones all of you together need to meet. Ask for their suggestions of ways they can contribute to making their season one in which they peak when it is time to do so.

The Streak

When the information that keeps coming into awareness is congruent with goals, psychic energy flows effortlessly. There is no need to worry, no reason to question one's adequacy. But whenever one does stop to think about oneself, the evidence is encouraging: "You are doing all right." The positive feedback strengthens the self, and more attention is freed to deal with the outer and inner environment.

—Mihaly Csikszentmihalyi,
Flow: The Psychology of Optimal Experience

> **Caution! The following contains many explicit stories about the sordid details of basketball games. Non-coaches should sample with care!**

The Streak began on January 18, 1996 with a victory over Los Altos.

January 18, 1996—Los Altos at Fremont

I have been depressed over our slow start in league all week. At one point I had a strange memory of a Friday afternoon in 1978 or 1979 when I was working for the Oregon Department of Energy. ODOE, as we affectionately called it, was housed in the attic of the old Garfield School a couple of blocks from the Capital Mall in Salem. Often the attic was hot, and this particular day it was especially so. I was lethargic and couldn't seem to get myself going even though I had plenty of work to do. Finally I challenged myself to work as hard as I could for 30 minutes and then go home since I wasn't getting anything done anyway.

The most amazing thing happened. When I next looked at the clock it was nearly 6 P.M., and I was the only person left in the office. I had been concentrating intently for more than three hours without even realizing it. Later, as I analyzed what had happened, I realized that by limiting myself to having to focus for only 30 minutes, I had accidently freed up a tremendous reservoir of energy. Over time I realized there were great possibilities in this technique. An individual can put up with a lot of discomfort and even pain so long as he knows it is for a clearly delineated, limited amount of time.

I have used this principal many times in the intervening years and I called upon it once again in the locker room before the Los Altos game. I wrote on the chalkboard "10-9-8-7-6-5-4-3-2-1." I told the players that we had only ten games left in the season. In order to be able to put ourselves in a position to win the league title we needed to win nine of those ten games. I acknowledged that we might win nine of ten, or even ten of ten (one game being a non-league game), and still not win the league because Palo Alto was undefeated at this point and we have three losses. But if we were able to win nine of ten, we had a good shot at the title.

I asked them to put out of their minds the heart-breaking losses to Mountain View and Palo Alto and give everything they had to these next (and last) ten games.

I also reminded them that I would have to leave before the game ended to catch a plane to Boston to participate in a seminar at the Harvard Business School. I felt bad about leaving but was also excited about the seminar. I hoped in November when I agreed to go to Harvard that we would be able to handle Los Altos early and the game would be in hand by the time I had to leave. Our pregame visualization took a turn for the fanciful as I guided them through an experience of flying (see Chapter 7, p. 144).

We unveiled our pressure defense and it effectively ended the game in the first four minutes. Jenny got three baskets off steals and ended the first quarter with 13 points. We were up 21-10 at the end of the first, 36-19 at the half. I left toward the end of the third quarter after having instructed Leticia to leave Jenny in if she had a chance at the school record for points. I later found out that she scored 35, breaking Colleen's record of 30 from last year. We are now three-three in league.

January 20, 1996 — Saratoga at Fremont

In the locker room before the game, I gave Jenny the chalk and asked her to put a line through the 10. This could be the beginning of a ritual. After each game the player that contributes the most to the win gets to cross out the number for that game. I need to make sure the numbers aren't erased between games. Tonight when I went into the locker room before the game I found that the numbers had been erased. I wrote new numbers up and tried to make them look like the original numbers. Call me superstitious, but I don't want anything to get in the way of our building self-confidence.

Saratoga played us closer than Los Altos but again our pressure defense got us a number of easy baskets and kept them out of their offense. In fact, I realized after the game that I didn't even know what their offense was because they rarely got to set up in the half-court.

Haruka hit four three-pointers in the first half and we were up by nine at halftime. We ended up doubling them 56-28. Four and three in League!

January 25, 1996 — Fremont at Santa Clara

We dodged a bullet against Santa Clara. They had beaten us earlier in the year when Colleen was sick, Natalie was gone, and Karen was injured. We actually led them at halftime, but with only six players—not all of them healthy—we ran out of gas in the second half. This time we were at full strength but still trailed by nine at halftime. I embarrassed myself by getting a technical foul toward the end of the first half for trying to "help" the referees make the right calls. Although I probably got some calls at first, eventually one of the refs got tired of it and called me for a technical. At the half I tried to talk to him and he just turned away, saying that I had "disrespected" them the entire first half. As I thought about it, I realized he was right. It was disrespectful to be yelling out traveling and other calls when that was their job. It came as a shock to realize that my wanting to win so much had seduced me, once again into crossing the line into coaching behaviors that I found detestable when I saw them in others.

I apologized to the players in the locker room and then sought out the referee at the beginning of the second half. Before he could walk away again I quickly said "Look, you were right. I'm sorry. I made a mistake and I won't do it again." He seemed a little taken aback, then shook my hand, and we started the second half with me keeping a zipper on my mouth.

Great shooting and superior conditioning rescued us. Haruka hit three three-pointers in a row late in the third quarter. At one point in a time-out, I started to sub for Haruka to give her a rest and Jenny said "Don't do that, she's hot." So I didn't. Natalie made an amazing line-drive layup that rattled the entire backboard, clanged against the rim but somehow went through the net. Jenny scored 19 of her 25 points in the second half, and Haruka scored all 11 of her points after the half. I alternated Natalie and Chi on their point guard, trying to deny her the ball. Amazingly, we were able to go several minutes down the stretch without letting her touch the ball. When other people were handling the ball for them they didn't often score. While we were increasing our intensity, they seemed to be running out of gas. We won 58-53. Whew! I'm glad we don't have to play them again.

After the game I told Ron Ingram, whom I've known and liked since we coached against each other in Cupertino Hoops, that I thought he had the strongest team in the league (after us) and that I sure hoped they would beat Palo Alto because we couldn't catch them simply by winning all the rest of our games. Then our two teams could share the league championship. He said that would be nice and that he had told his players in the locker room not to be too down about the loss because he thought we were the best team in the league in spite of our record. Five-three in league!

January 27, 1996 — Sacred Heart Cathedral at Fremont

After our thrilling near-miss against Sacred Heart Cathedral in the CCS playoffs last year, I decided to try to schedule a late-season game with them to serve as a tune-up for the playoffs. The game began well enough. We started in our Scramble defense and Jenny stole the ball at midcourt and went in for a layup but missed. Colleen had a couple of open short shots that also just wouldn't drop. Chi had a steal and missed the layup. Nonetheless, we were with them through the first half and I was feeling that we could easily have been ahead if we had made those easy baskets. In the second half, SHC just wore us out with their own pressure and ran away from us, beating us badly.

I was disappointed, but not overly so. SHC's guards were very quick and took advantage of our young ball handlers. I have no doubt that Chi and Natalie, both sophomores, will be much more prepared for quick guards in the playoffs because of this game. Still I wasn't sure what to say in the locker room. Fortunately I didn't have to worry about it because when I opened the discussion Shauna immediately said "I know we're all disappointed that we lost this game. But we're doing really well in league and I think we should look at this as a practice game designed to help us get better, and not get discouraged." Heads nodding all around the locker room.

I couldn't have said it better!

January 30, 1996 — Wilcox at Fremont

Our first game against Wilcox several weeks ago was total schizophrenia. It was as if two totally different teams came out for the second half. They won the first half 35-19. We won the second half 36-9 and the game 55-44. Wasn't sure what to expect this time. I needn't have worried. Wilcox had trouble with our pressure defense and we defeated them 44-25. Six-three in league.

February 2, 1996 — Fremont at Palo Alto

Last night will be hard to top. Jeff McKay wanted to see me coach a game and this one fit into his busy schedule. We had dinner together and then he sat on the bench with me during the first half of the game. I always feel that he thinks I'm a better coach than I really am. Tonight was the perfect time for him to see a game because I want him to continue to think that way! Everything clicked.

Here's how the *Palo Alto Daily News* described it.

Put simply, the Fremont of Sunnyvale girls' basketball team came into Palo Alto last night and beat the host Vikings, 63-41.

Put with more complexity, the loss leads to self-doubt for the Vikings.

Was it simply a case of Fremont playing at the top of its game? Or was it a sign of something greater, that Palo Alto may be in danger of losing its season-long grip on first place in the Santa Clara Valley Athletic League El Camino Division?

Only Paly's final four El Camino games will tell for sure. With the disappointing defeat, the Vikings (15-7, 8-2 in SCVAL play) fell into a tie for first with Santa Clara, 68-50 winners over Cupertino. Fremont moved to within one game of the top at 7-3, 8-12 overall. . .

Fremont used a 1-2-2 press to repeatedly and effectively trap Palo Alto at the halfcourt line. Without point guard Mia Sibug, who sat out with an air cast on her sprained right ankle, the vikings were unable to dribble through the inevitable double-teams, and their passes to the wings were picked off far too often to win.

"Their defense was really, really good," said sophomore guard Tiffany Mok, who led Paly with 12 points. "We weren't prepared for the type of defense they were playing us, and the absence of Mia wasn't helping us when they had a defense we hadn't handled before. I must commend them for their defense."

Fremont forced Paly into 23 turnovers, including 13 in a first half that saw the Vikings fall behind 34-18. According to coach Jim Thompson, use of the halfcourt trap was designed not only to help on defense but also on offense.

"We've been a little passive on defense much of the year," Thompson said. "By going to the trap, it makes us more aggressive. . . In previous games, we started in a man-to-man and then went to the trap, but today we started (in the trap) right away because I wanted to be aggressive from the start."

. . . the Vikings were so scrambled by the press that they weren't able to take advantage of their decided size advantage on the low block. . . Palo Alto never stopped Smith, who finished with a game-high 24 points,* nor Jenny White (20 points), who kept getting open for fast-break layups courtesy of steals from the pressing defense.

---

*Colleen ended up with her photo in the sports pages after being named the player of the week by the *San Jose Mercury News*.

Despite the obvious deficiencies his club had pointed out in Paly's game, Thompson still feels the Vikings are in the driver's seat.

"This was our best game, period," Thompson said. "Palo Alto is a really good team . . . Santa Clara has two losses and Palo Alto has two losses. We still need somebody to beat them."

This is the kind of game you want to savor for a long time! Seven-three in league.

February 6, 1996 — Mountain View at Fremont

Caught a break in that Mountain View's top player, Jen Santos, was under the weather. Again our defense made the difference and I didn't even realize that she hadn't scored until she made a freethrow late in the third quarter.

I think I overreacted to the charge that I had run up the score against Palo Alto and started subbing earlier than I should have. I started subbing early in the second half and kept the starters on the bench even when the scored closed to 12 points. Fortunately, they never got any closer and we won 60-45. Eight-three in league.

Saratoga came within one point of Palo Alto tonight, 43-42. Too bad. Paly and Santa Clara both still need to lose one more for us to tie them.

February 8, 1996 — Fremont at Los Altos

Tonight was Los Altos' last home game. Whoever did the scheduling did them no favors. They play both of their last two games away. There was a little ceremony for the two seniors. As soon as it was over, I told my players in the huddle "See how happy they are. Let's make this the last happy moment of the evening for them." Everyone laughed. Afterwards I felt a little bit guilty about being so hardcore, but it was pretty much that way. We handled them easily and Amalia played especially well, finally getting a chance to play for an extended period of time. She ended up with four rebounds, three points, and two steals, which reflected how hard she was working on defense. In some ways the game was not good for us because we couldn't use our pressure defense for most of the game or the score would have gotten way out of control. Not so good with two tough games next week. Nonetheless, nine-three in league!

And then when I called the *Mercury News* to check on the Cupertino-Palo Alto game, I got the terrific news that Cupertino had squeaked past Paly 50-46. We are now tied with Paly and Santa Clara for the league lead—something that would have seemed unthinkable just a few weeks ago.

February 10, 1996

I came home from practice exhausted and drifted off to sleep on the couch, only to be awakened about 10 by numerous phone calls from excited parents and players. The first call came from Georgi, Jenny's mom. She and Colleen's parents had gone to see Santa Clara play at Wilcox. It turns out that Wilcox won on a three-pointer at the buzzer, 45-43. After they got home and told their kids, the players started calling each other and (repeatedly) me. So now it's just us and Palo Alto and, if Santa Clara can beat Paly next week, it might just be us.

February 13, 1996 — Fremont at Saratoga

This turned out to be a tough game against a pretty good team with a terrible record. They are well-coached and will be strong next year. I'm not sure why they haven't won more games. They sure play us tough.

In retrospect I realize I wasn't very alert. I think the pressure of having to win every game to have a chance for the league title is getting to me. I saw Saratoga during warm-ups taking the ball into one corner and then skip-passing it to the other corner and dumping it inside to their huge post player. But I didn't register it and they were able to do that same maneuver against our traps repeatedly in the first half. This was the first time since we had implemented our Scramble trapping defense that it wasn't working. Finally, I called it off and we went back to our basic half-court defense, and that kept them from getting the ball into the post where they had such a height advantage. We completely stopped them from scoring during a long period in the third quarter. Early in the fourth quarter, on successive possessions, Haruka and then Chi stole the ball and went in for lay-ups. That pretty much settled it and we pulled away for a 49-40 victory.

I talked with Phil Kelly, who had been at the game. If I had known he was there, I would have asked his advice at the time. He said that going back to our basic defense was a good move. "Whenever something isn't working, always go back to the basics and get back to sound fundamental basketball. Then you can venture out again once you've got the basics working." Good advice. I still have a lot to learn about coaching. It's amazing how complicated a simple game like basketball can be!

Santa Clara put up a good fight but lost to Palo Alto 52-45. Too bad. But I guess I shouldn't be greedy. A few weeks ago it looked like our season was going into the tank, and now I'm not satisfied to be tied with Paly.

Ten-three in league! Only one to go now.

February 15, 1996 — Cupertino at Fremont

Tonight we were on the other end of the elaborate ceremony for the seniors that we saw at Los Altos. I was concerned because there was so much emotion. The six girls who were graduating (Amalia, Colleen, Haruka, Jenny, Karen, and Shauna) had contributed so much to the school for so many years. And I knew how each of them must feel about their last home game. Just as I feared, we came out tight and got behind 14-5 at the first quarter. But the team didn't panic and I never felt worried. I believe this was a situation where our catastrophization visualization (see Chapter 7, p. 142) came to our rescue. I think the girls had so much confidence in their ability by this time that they knew that if they kept playing their game they would win.

We outscored them 22-5 in the second quarter and finished with a 45-37 victory. Two school records fell tonight. Haruka hit two more three-pointers to give her 38 for the season* and Colleen collected 19 rebounds for the best single-game performance. This was perfect because Jenny had broken Colleen's school single-game scoring record earlier in the season. Now each of our three top players owns a school record.

Afterward, we all stood under the "Girls Basketball League Champions" banner and pointed up to it while what seemed like

*She got three more in the CCS playoff game to finish with 41.

hundreds of parents took pictures of us. I made a makeshift sign that said "1996" and one of the girls held that up toward the banner. No one wanted to leave the gym. We had all worked so hard for so long that it was just so sweet to be there and soak in the feeling of having done what we had committed ourselves to do back in mid-January. Nine league wins in a row, a record of 11-3 in league and no worse than tied for first in league, depending on how Palo Alto did tonight.*

Eventually the janitor asked me to help persuade people to leave so he could clean the gym and go home.

*Palo Alto nipped Wilcox 52-49 so we share the title. I've gotten beyond my greed. I'm more than satisfied..

Chapter 7

Tall Trees and Catastrophes: Visualization and Transformation

Images have their own potency and their own persistence; they testify to human need and desire, but also to a transcendent frontier that marks either a limit to the human, or a limitlessness that may be beyond the human.

—Harold Bloom, **Omens of Millennium**

When Is a Door Not a Door?

There is a team-building activity in which the leaders of two groups are presented with a design that requires their groups to replicate by collaboration, using two long loops of rope. There are two catches: only the two leaders get to see the design and everyone, including the leaders, is blindfolded before the exercise begins.

Recently, I participated in this activity with a group of my MBA students. We had done this the year before so I took the role of blindfolded follower and settled in passively to do as I was told, determined not to use my previous experience to shortcut the group's problem-solving process.

At first, as you might expect, there was mass confusion. The two leaders who had seen the design tried to communicate what they wanted the rest of us to do. There was much frustration. Finally Michael, one of the leaders, hit upon an image with which we all were familiar. He told us that what we wanted to do was create a "patio door that is one-quarter open."

As I listened to Michael I became conflicted. It was clear to me that he was giving the group bad information. The design was really supposed to be two diamonds that intersected to create a smaller diamond. I finally decided that I needed to challenge his directions. When I did, he was very clear that the design was a patio door and Leah, the other leader, concurred. At that point it occurred to me that the facilitators for this exercise from Catalyst Consulting had changed the rules and I was operating from an outdated image.

With the shared vision of a partly opened patio door clear in our heads, we were able to place the two ropes to successfully complete the assignment well within the 30 minutes we were given.

Afterwards, I had to laugh as I remembered an old joke from my boyhood: "When is a door not a door? Answer: When it's a jar." Michael had brought that joke full circle with his vivid image of a patio door that really was ajar!

How often groups are unable to work together because they don't have a common vision! Often, vision is used merely in a figurative sense. When people talk about corporate vision, they usually don't *literally* mean a picture or an image that is shared. What was so helpful about Michael's direction was that each of us could clearly see *exactly* what he was talking about. Because it was a literal image, we were able to get the job done with a minimum of confusion, miscommunication and conflict. Getting the right picture in people's heads was half the battle. Once we all could clearly see that patio door in spite of our blindfolds, we could use our creative energy productively, comfortable in the knowledge that we all were addressing the same problem.

Cool Water in a Hot Wagon

This experience reminded me of a story told by Andrew Young in his book *An Easy Burden*, about an ingenious application of visualization during the early years of the Civil Rights Movement. A group of civil rights workers had been arrested during a march in Savannah in 1962.

Before the march, Young was concerned about the discipline of the group. The marchers had not been adequately trained in the theory and practice of nonviolence and were not prepared for the kind of violence that might be directed toward them on the march. They were arrested and, after a night in jail, the group was loaded onto a paddy wagon, 20 protesters in a wagon meant to hold no more than eight.

> It was already hot and humid and the tiny windows were partially obstructed with metal bars across them. The crowd magnified the heat; it was like being in an oven. The kids in my paddy wagon panicked and started yelling, 'it's hot, let us out of here!' The response of the police was to close the windows: now there was no air circulating.

Eventually the heat and close quarters began to wear on the protesters as the police intended, hoping to break the spirit of the group. Young had to think fast.

> I said very calmly and quietly, "Look, they are trying to get you to crack up. They want you to scream and holler and plead. That would demonstrate that you are niggers who got out of your place. They will have punished you and put you back in your place and you'll be a good nigger for a long, long time. You can't let this get you down. You've got to use mind over matter." Then I said, "Everybody close your eyes, we're going to the beach. It's hot, we're sweating. All the sweat is dripping off of us, but we're almost to the water. We've got about ten more steps to the water. When you put yourself in the water, it's going to be cold, it's going to send shivers down your spine, and you're going to wonder whether you want to get in the water, but we're going in. We're going to wade in the water." I "walked" them out into the water until it was about waist deep. Then I said, "Let's sing about it." We started singing soft as a whisper, "Wade in the water, wade in the water, children." When the police officers heard us singing, they realized we weren't going to crack up, and they let us out. . .

Visualization is also gaining advocates in the healing professions. My mother has suffered from debilitating migraines for many years. Recently, she saw a therapist who gave her a mental technique to use whenever she felt a migraine coming on. I assumed that the doctor had given her some kind of meditation exercise. Later, I discovered that he had asked her where in the world she felt the most relaxed and comfortable. She told him about her cabin on Lake Sallie in Minnesota. The therapist asked her to close her eyes and imagine herself at Lake Sallie at the onset of a migraine. This technique has given her a powerful tool to deal with headaches. Whereas she formerly was laid low for a couple of days from a migraine, she now is usually able to derail the experience with her visualization of the soothing beauty of Lake Sallie.

Visualization and Memory

Visualization has long been a powerful memory tool. *The Memory Palace of Matteo Ricci*, Jonathan Spence's story of a Western traveler in 16th-century China, describes how visualization can help an individual memorize vast amounts of material. Ricci visualized the various rooms in his palace and placed items he wanted to remember in the palace in the order he would encounter them. Amy Tan similarly describes a visualization technique for how a woman with a so-called photographic memory recalls a number in *The Hundred Secret Senses*:

> If someone asked me what my address was when I was seven years old, the numbers wouldn't flash before my eyes. I'd have to relive a specific moment: the heat of the day, the smell of the cut lawn, the slap-slap-slap of rubber thongs against my heels. Then once again I'd be walking up the two steps of the poured-concrete porch, reaching into the black mailbox, heart pounding, fingers grasping—Where is it? Where's that stupid letter from Art Linkletter, inviting me to be on his show? But I wouldn't give up hope. I'd think to myself, Maybe I'm at the wrong address. But no, there they are, the brass numbers above, 3-6-2-4, complete with tarnish and rust around the screws.

These examples portray a truth of visualization, namely that it is not just a seeing experience. For visualization to be effective, it should engage as many of the senses as possible. In effect, simply seeing is not believing. The effective visualizer inhabits the situation she is trying to imagine so as to be able to perfect a particular technique.

Visualization has been around for a long time. Recently it has become the focus of a lot of attention by those who want to improve performance, initially in sports, but more and more in business as well.

Drivers of Transformation

About the time I was starting to coach at Fremont I heard a speaker quote Carl Jung to the effect that transformation in the absence of images is impossible. I took this to mean that marginal, incremental changes can be made quite readily, but transformational kinds of changes need the vividness of an image to power them.

There is a favorite story from Paul Reps' classic *Zen Flesh, Zen Bones* that illustrates the transformative powers of visualization. It concerns a wrestler named O-nami, or "Great Waves," who is unbeatable in practice but is so shy that he cannot win matches in public. He consults a wandering Zen teacher named Hakuju, who may have been the very first sports psychologist: "Great waves is your name . . . so stay in this temple tonight. Imagine that you are those billows. You are no longer a wrestler who is afraid. You are those huge waves sweeping everything before them, swallowing all in their path. Do this and you will be the greatest wrestler in the land."

O-nami spends the night thus: "He thought of many different things. Then gradually he turned more and more to the feeling of the waves. As the night advanced the waves became larger and larger. They swept away the flowers in their vases. Even the Buddha in the shrine was inundated. Before dawn the temple was nothing but the ebb and flow of an immense sea." O-nami thus became a champion.

In one sense vivid images serve as the equivalent of a road map. You might think about traveling around your own neighborhood. Since you are not far from home and you know the area, it is possible without a map to find a new store even if you're not exactly sure where it is. However, traveling to an exotic locale, one you have never explored, you would be lost without a map or its equivalent.

I began to think about visualization (literally seeing images) as a powerful driver of transformation, one that I wanted to explore with my players.

Journal Entry—December 8, 1994

A nice thing happened in practice the other day. I have been a little uneasy about the visualization exercises I have been having the players do. They haven't said much about them and I just didn't know how they felt about doing them. No one has really complained about it and the giggling from the first few times has disappeared, but I still am insecure about it. But yesterday, Colleen told me that they had talked about visualization in her psychology class. The teacher had told her "You know, this could help you in basketball." Colleen said she replied "I know, like, we're already doing it." The teacher told her "Wow, that's pretty advanced stuff for a high school team." Made me feel good to get that reinforcement from an unexpected source and it was clear that Colleen thought it was pretty cool too.

Introducing Visualization

I had become interested in visualization several years earlier and used it successfully to improve my performance in such diverse performing arts as public speaking and bowling. But this was my first opportunity to try it out on a team determined to perform at a high level.

While I have a lot of confidence *now* in my ability to use visualization effectively with young athletes, I was insecure and tentative about it the first few times I tried it with my players. I want people to respect me, and I was nervous about asking my players to do something they might think was weird.

However, I am fascinated by the practical challenges of implementing good ideas in a way that will work in a specific situation. Over the years I have learned that I can persevere even while feeling afraid or foolish. And my experience has tended to reinforce my experimental tendencies, since more often than not it all works out pretty well.

So, in spite of uncomfortable feelings, I began gradually to introduce visualization to my players. I acknowledged to them that it might seem silly at first but that many of the top athletes in the world attributed part of their success to the practice of visualization. I tried not to oversell the technique. Although I believe it can make a significant difference, visualization doesn't obviate the need for having some talent to start with, practicing hard and effectively, and being on the receiving end of some plain, old luck—having the ball bounce your way at opportune times.

I shared my own experience and success with visualization and told my players of an experiment I had read about in which young basketball players were divided into three groups. The first group practiced free-throws for a set period of time every day. The second group only visualized shooting free throws for the same amount of time every day. The third group practiced shooting *and* visualized. At the end of the experiment, as might be expected, the third group did much better than either of the other two. However, what was surprising was that the visualization-only group did almost as well as the group that actually shot free throws.

I believed strongly in the power of visualization in the context of a well-designed practice regimen, but my experience base was small and my discomfort level still exceedingly high during the first few times I guided my players through visualization exercises. I probably never would have gotten into visualization in a big way with the team as things stood at that time. Fortunately, psychological reinforcement was close at hand.

I had developed a lecture on the "Technology of Self-Confidence" and delivered it to my Learning to Lead students. Among the confidence-building techniques I discussed was visualization. After class, one of my students, Juliet Thompson Hochman, approached me. As a member of the 1988 U.S. Olympic Rowing Team she had used visualization extensively to prepare herself for competition.

She confirmed my own experience and readings. Visualization had been a powerful tool for her in her successful quest to become a world-class rower and make the Olympic Team. She offered to share her experiences with my players, which made for a fascinating session. Juliet told my spellbound players that when she finally marched into the Olympic Stadium in Seoul, Korea, it was exactly as she knew it would be because she had done it thousands of times in her mind as she lay in bed every night.

She also talked about how she prepared for what was the hardest part of the race for her—waiting for all the boats to get lined up for the start. She would be all keyed up and ready to race and then would have to wait for an uncertain period of time, all the while maintaining her readiness to give it everything she had the moment the starter's gun went off. This reminded me of a nefarious tactic of coaches who call a timeout when an opposing player has to shoot an important free throw, just to give them time to think about it, in the hope that it will raise just a hair of doubt in the player's mind.

Juliet described how she regularly visualized herself sitting in her boat waiting for the start. She would feel the sensation of discomfort at having to sit still when she was ready to go and deal with the uncertainty of when the gun would sound. She would visualize herself *dealing with* the discomfort and uncertainty and being ready with her best effort when the race began.

Juliet's involvement at this point was crucial for me because of my own insecurities. Her endorsement of the technique gave me the courage to plunge ahead in the face of the inevitable discomfort that accompanies the use of the nontraditional.

Rehearsing Perfect Performance

After Juliet spoke to my players, I left my inhibitions about visualization behind. We began to visualize several times a week. The night before a game I encouraged the girls to take advantage of the time in bed before they fell asleep to visualize how they wanted to perform the next night.

Usually we visualized at or near the end of practice. Often the boys' varsity team would come into the gym right before we would end. We would practice on the floor for the last possible moment before the court belonged to the boys. Then I would take the team over to one corner of the gymnasium and bunch everyone close together on the bleachers, have them get comfortable with both feet on the floor, and close their eyes.

I actually found the distraction of the noisy boys helpful in setting the stage. "In a game there will be all kinds of distractions, so let's focus our attention internally and leave the noise at the other end of the gym behind." Then I would describe the situation and ask the players to see what I was describing.

Initially our visualization exercises fell into a category called "rehearsal of perfect performance." An athlete sees herself in the competitive situation in which she wants to perform well. She smells, feels, hears, touches, and sees the situation with as much richness as she is able. She then sees herself performing the physical act perfectly.

I encouraged the players to use both an internal and an external camera. The "external camera" shows the visualizer what she looks like when she is performing, as if she were viewing a videotape of her performance after the fact. The "internal camera" is the experience as the athlete *sees* it through her own eyes. She doesn't see herself; she sees what she will see when she does what she is visualizing.

Both techniques have their benefits and I believed that learning to do both helped develop the "visualization muscle" in my players. By visualizing themselves through the external camera, they were forced to develop a mental blueprint of the proper motion of a free throw or a block-out that could serve as a constant comparison to what they actually did on the floor in practice or a game. The internal camera was crucial because it was more realistic. It was, after all, what they would experience at the time of performance.

In the beginning, we mostly visualized the mechanics of individual tasks such as shooting and rebounding. Over time, I began to ask them to visualize our defensive coordination as a team, especially as our defense became more complex. I wanted them to see themselves moving aggressively to fill the vulnerabilities in our press. I asked them to see where each of their teammates were on the floor and where they were moving to as the other team took the ball out of bounds. I would usually start our full-court press visualization with us scoring and each of them jumping aggressively to their position since nothing destroys a press as quickly as having forgetful players trot happily downcourt after we score.

Over time, as we tried to move away from a set-play offense to a more free-wheeling motion offense, I began to guide the players through the various offensive options they could use in response to what the defense did.

I believe the beginning of a game is usually the most nerve-wracking for players. It often sets a tone for the entire game that can be hard to recover from if things don't go well. I began asking the players to visualize the opening few plays of the upcoming game. This led inevitably to our pre-game visualizations in the locker room.

Our pregame and half-time visualizations probably got started by a remark my wife made after a traumatic loss to Cupertino High School. We shot about as poorly in the first half of that game as is possible, making only two out of twenty-eight shots. Until I looked at the shot chart after the game I just couldn't understand what the problem was.

Afterwards, I realized that we were getting good shots—we just weren't hitting any.

My mother asked me what I said to the girls at half-time. I didn't have any insightful comments to make and admitted that. Sandra suggested that the next time we have a really bad shooting night, I might have the girls close their eyes and relax rather than simply talk at them. She reasoned that they were probably nervous and relaxation might be the best thing to do. That gave me the idea to try visualizing in the locker room before games, during half-time, and even briefly during timeouts. In time, our pre-game visualizations became an important part of our routine.

Catastrophization

Rehearsal of perfect performance is a pretty straightforward technique. There is a more emotionally sophisticated variation, sometimes called *catastrophization* that involves visualizing a situation in which pretty much everything goes wrong. Catastrophization involves visualizing yourself prevailing in a worst-case scenario. I became interested in catastrophization, appropriately enough, through experiencing a minor catastrophe of my own.

In March 1994 I gave a six-hour workshop to a group of physical education teachers in nearby Sequoia Union School District. Shortly after I began, a gentleman whom I shall call Mr. Gruff sprang up and shouted something aggressively challenging like "What is your point? Is there some purpose for your being here?" I was shaken but managed to stammer "Just wait and I think you'll see." I had seen "harumpf" in print but the first time I ever heard it spoken was by Mr. Gruff as he sat down briefly before dramatically stomping out moments later.

This was minute two of a six-hour workshop! If time flies when you are having fun, this may have been the longest day of my life. Somehow I made it through the day. Several people even complimented me afterwards, and one or two apologized for Mr. Gruff's behavior. I was emotionally exhausted but decided that I had handled the situation with a certain amount of grace. What does not kill you makes you stronger. Nonetheless I was determined *never* to find myself unprepared for that kind of a situation again.

Since then, I have rarely given an important presentation without preparing by envisioning the worst that might happen. The goal of this kind of visualization is to truly experience the awful emotions when our best-laid plans turn to mush *without* allowing the feelings to incapacitate us. In catastrophization, we continue the visualization to the point where we persevere *through* the bad times and ultimately prevail. For example, often a team will get behind early and fall apart emotionally, so that instead of rallying and getting back in a game that is still winnable, it gives up.

I knew that often it is the psychological rather than the physical aspect of the game that is the debilitating culprit. Catastrophization is designed to show players that they have the ability to persevere and recover and not be dissuaded by emotional discomfort.

A typical catastrophization exercise would begin with me describing the beginning of a game in which everything goes wrong. For example, the other team gets the jump and quickly drives for a lay-up. They then steal the in-bounds pass and score. Then one of our players is called for a charging foul and our opponent drives once again down the court to score. Before we know what hit us, we are way behind.

I asked the girls to experience that awful feeling of being crushed right at the start. I asked them to sit with that feeling so they would not forget how it felt. Then I asked them to feel their own determination welling up inside them. Sometimes I was rewarded by seeing a girl's jaw clench with determination at this point as she visualized. I asked them to visualize themselves making renewed efforts in spite of the discouraged feelings they felt. They continued to feel the awful feelings but still tried even harder and came up with the next loose ball, the next steal, the next rebound, the next three-point basket.

I also told them stories about other athletes who had prevailed over horrible beginnings. Marathoner Nancy Ditz told a reporter in 1987 how she prepared for the intense heat of the Los Angeles Marathon. "In her mind's eye, she saw herself remaining calm and not wasting vital energy worrying about things she couldn't control. As it turned out, her water bottle wasn't available at one point during the race. And Ditz remained calm as she had visualized she would." She went on to win the L.A. Marathon in spite of her discomfort running in the heat and her worst fear having occurred.

This is similar to something the twelve-step movement calls "acting as if." You act as if you are successful until it comes true. I remember reading about a young man named Bobby Zimmerman, facing his booing, disdainful classmates in Hibbing, Minnesota, singing *as if* he were a famous singer—which he became after changing his name to Dylan. The image in his head allowed him to transcend his critics and bring great music to the world.

Tall Trees and Other Flights of Imagination

Much of the literature on visualization for sports focuses on getting the mechanics right—for example, having players see themselves making a free throw with perfect form.

As the 1995–96 season progressed, I began to get a little bit bored with the mechanical aspects of visualization and to drift into a more imaginistic strain of visualization. I felt I was repeating myself during both practice and pre-game visualizations and was ready for something else. One night, as we prepared to do our pre-game visualization before playing Los Altos, I suddenly had the image in my mind of our players floating through the air. Perhaps this was due to having recently seen the Cirque du Soleil's performance of *Allegria*, with its mystical images of flight. It may also have been connected to my dreams. For years I have had a recurring dream in which I am able to fly. Going with the image of flight, I abandoned the instrumental, literal rehearsal kind of visualization I had planned and asked them to imagine that they could lift their arms above their waists and cause themselves to float off the ground.

There was a bit of giggling, since this was not the kind of "practical" visualization they were used to. We spent the next few minutes floating up to grab rebounds, flying to the top of the gymnasium to dunk alley-oop passes from each other. When they lifted their hands above their waists, they floated up. To descend, they simply brought their arms below their waists. After a few minutes of this, we came back to reality and went out and trounced our opponents.

Since that new kind of visualization had been fun, *and* we handily had won the game, I was emboldened to try something similar the next game. I felt the need to do something a bit different rather than simply repeat the same exercise.

I continued the flying imagery but asked them to see themselves as eagles. Again they soared, but this time I asked them to use the internal camera and see their wings as they soared and dived. I assured them that they had wonderful telescopic eyesight with which they spied an orange object way down below. They dived and snatched the object with their claws and brought it back to their nest, in which their eaglets eagerly awaited the next meal. When they examined their prize they discovered it was a basketball. They tossed it into the nest and encouraged their babies to ball-fake each time before they passed it to one of their siblings (we were getting too many passes intercepted because we telegraphed them and I could not pass up a single opportunity to reinforce the idea of ball-faking!).

By the next game the girls eagerly awaited the pre-game visualization. The Fremont student body was in the process of voting for a replacement mascot for the Indian, and wolves constituted 40% of the choices ("The Wolfpack" and "Lobos" being two of the five choices). I experimented with the team's visualizing themselves as a pack of wolves hunting a deer through the snowy forest at night. This got a little bloody as we weren't visualizing basketballs this time. I even had the wolves predigest the food (as real wolves do) for their pups before they regurgitated it for them. I decided afterwards that I might have gone too far with the realism here, so when I used wolves again I omitted the bringing-down-the-deer scenario. But the image of a pack of wolves rolling through a forest at night was a powerful one that I returned to for another game.*

For one visualization exercise I had the girls become wolves returning from the hunt to find a huge and powerful wolverine threatening their young in their den. Because of the size and ferocity of the wolverine, the pack needed to work together to drive him off, which fortunately they were able to do without bloodletting.

For our second Palo Alto game I wanted something special, since Palo Alto was leading the league at that time. I remembered that a tall tree is the symbol of the city of Palo Alto, so I asked the girls to become a tiny seedling that grew and grew and grew until it towered over the landscape. By looking down with their tree-eyes they spied a tiny little

---

*I was so taken with this image that I was disappointed when the student body chose the "Firebirds" as the new mascot in the spring of 1996. As it turned out, I needn't have worried!

vehicle driving up to their trunk. By squinting they were able to see that the school bus had green and white letters on the side saying "Palo Alto." Then some very tiny girls (this was quite amusing to my team because Palo Alto had some huge players!) got out and tried to chop down the tree with their tiny, tiny axes, to no avail. The girls felt themselves as incredibly strong and the axes as no more than little pinpricks because they were so big and powerful.

Perhaps my most inspired visualization came before our game with Wilcox. For some reason I was feeling nostalgic (perhaps I was psychic!). I had the girls see and feel themselves many years in the future as grandmothers rocking in their dotage. I asked them to feel the arthritis in their aching bones and the wrinkled skin on their faces and hands. Then their granddaughter, who happened to be a basketball player, came in and asked them about the good old days when they were basketball stars and especially about the night they destroyed Wilcox High School. It was especially thrilling that they then went out and did what they had visualized.

The Coach as Visualizer

The coach's primary role in visualization is tour guide, the narrator who sets the stage, the one who helps the performers get the most of their ability. But coaching is also a demanding performing art in its own right. Coaches must make real-time decisions with consequences for their teams. I already described how I use catastrophization to prepare myself for situations such as important presentations in which I need to perform well under stress .

At some point I realized that I could use visualization to help me perform better as a coach. I began to visualize myself coaching the perfect game. I thought about what that would mean and came up with three elements of what perfect performance as a coach would look like: hyper-awareness, putting the needs of the players first, and respecting the referees.

Hyper-Awareness

There is a great line in the film *Phenomenon*, in which John Travolta plays a man who experiences a remarkable increase in brainpower. In one scene, he learns Portuguese while being driven to the home of a woman who speaks only Portugese by speedreading a Portuguese-English dictionary. When he is asked how he is able to learn so much so quickly, he says "I just see things so clearly now." Many of us have occasionally experienced this clarity, which I like to call hyper-awareness.

In our first Central Coast Section playoff game against King City in February 1995, I experienced this clarity. There was a moment in which I saw exactly what needed to be done and doing it helped us win the game. It was some time in the early part of the fourth quarter. We had come back from a nine-point deficit at half-time to tie the game. Jenny hit a basket and was fouled, to give us a two-point lead. As she went to the foul line, I had the experience of hyper-awareness. I saw the court and the game so clearly, without the distraction of being identified with the outcome. It was almost as if I were watching the game from a different psychological time zone.

I realized that the King City players were extremely tired. Haruka had been harassing their point guard all over the court and she was beat. At that moment, the King City team seemed to be at the point of demoralization. They had a healthy lead going into the locker room at half-time. Now the game was in danger of slipping away from them. Suddenly it was clear to me that we should reactivate our full-court press. We had tried it earlier in the game but abandoned it when a couple of key players got into foul trouble. I signaled the team to press after Jenny's free throw. She made it, giving us a three-point lead. We pressed on their in-bounds and the distress was almost palpable on the faces of their guards who had played the entire game. For practical purposes the game was over even though we had five or six minutes left to play. The press demoralized them as I had foreseen. I saw that because I was in a different, better place than I normally am when coaching a game.

Putting Players First

A second element of my visualization of perfect performance as a coach is to be completely supportive of the players and in touch with what they need emotionally *for that game* to play their best. This came from my wife's advice during the depths of our December 1995 horror show—the bleak month in which we lost all nine games we played. The night before our first league game with Cupertino, early in January, Sandra suggested that I might want to stop worrying so much about whether we would win the game and focus instead on the needs of the players. "What do they need from you to be able to play their best game?"

I concluded that perfect performance would include giving each of them individual attention, being aware of their contribution to the effort both on the court and the bench, and supporting them whether they succeeded or failed.

Respecting the Referees

The third element of perfect coaching performance also came from a suggestion from my wife. I had gotten my second technical foul of the season, which horrified me. I didn't want to *ever* get a technical foul. The previous year I had one and then vowed never to let that happen again. But here I was in my second season having gotten two in less than a month. (Was I in the midst of a geometric progression? Next year four fouls, the year after eight, then sixteen?!) Sandra suggested that I focus on coaching a game that I could be proud of, and that I should think about what that would mean with respect to how I responded to the referees, particularly when they made bad calls.

When I did my individual visualization to prepare for a game, I saw myself functioning in a state of hyper-awareness where I could see what was happening on the court, open to intuitive mental leaps that would help us perform better. I also visualized myself in tune with each player and saying just the right thing to reinforce her strong efforts and helping all of them get on the right track when things weren't going well for them. Finally, I saw myself appreciating the efforts of the referees, who were human beings struggling with a difficult job just as we were.

The Benefits of Visualization

For those skeptical of the benefits of visualization, perhaps believing it to be primarily a placebo, I can only reply that they may be correct. Although I believe that visualization helped us play better, the most correct and honest response is that I don't really know how much it contributed to our ultimate success. There was no control group of the same (or similar) non-visualizing players with which to compare. But that is often the case for practitioners. There is some evidence that visualization works for outstanding athletes—at least many of them say it helps them. That in itself is important.

The fact that something is a placebo is not necessarily an argument against its use. There is a great scene in the movie *Bull Durham* in which Crash Davis (played by Kevin Costner) tells Annie Savoy (played by Susan Saradon) that if a player believes that some weird behavior helps him play well, then it doesn't matter whether it makes sense to anyone else. (Rent the video if you want to know the particular behavior he was talking about!) If a player *thinks* it helps him, then it does. My players, like many athletes, believed that visualization helped them become better basketball players.

I saw this in a very moving way. Just before our last game of the regular season against Cupertino, when we needed to win to have a chance for the league title, Jenny asked me if I would repeat the "Tall Trees" visualization. I said I had planned something else and asked her why she wanted that one. She said it was the one we had used before our decisive win against Palo Alto. It had been successful then and Jenny (who was speaking on behalf of the team) wanted very much to be successful that night. I took that as the highest praise I could get from the players. In their minds, visualization had helped them beat a good team and they wanted to keep using it. Naturally I was not going to deny her request, so once again we were Tall Trees and once again we were successful.

In the absence of definitive proof, I nonetheless believe that visualization works for several reasons:

1. *Increased practice time.* Visualization results in more practice, and practice improves performance. In Chapter 5 I discussed our formula $S = E/T$, which stands for "success comes from effort over time." Simply put, visualization gives you more time. With every activity there is a physical limit to the amount of time you can practice. High schools and colleges have limits to how many hours a week teams can practice. Even if there are no regulations about length of practice times, there are physical constraints (such as access to practice facilities). The basketball court may not be open at 10 P.M. but the gym in the player's mind is ready for use as she lies in bed waiting to fall asleep.

Players in collision sports like football increase the likelihood of injury when they practice under contact conditions for a longer period of time.* Visualization provides an impact-free form of practice.

The key here is that visualizing improper technique may be no better than improper practice. If you are practicing something incorrectly, you are not likely to improve if you practice longer. I am reminded of how Roland Ortmayer, coach at the University of LaVerne, abruptly cancelled the rest of a practice because his players were doing so poorly. Some of his players ventured that perhaps if they were doing so poorly they should practice more rather than less. He retorted that they were simply reinforcing their bad habits rather than learning proper performance. Rehearsing improper performance is not likely to result in improvement.

2. *Boredom relief.* Visualization relieves the boredom of practicing and drilling. It simply isn't possible to refine technique without lots and lots of repetitions. And repetition often leads to boredom. Visualization offers a way for players to get more reps in the magical privacy of their own imagination. Juliet Thompson Hochman imagined herself in the Olympics. I remember a boyhood in which I spent hundreds of hours throwing a ball against the back wall of Our Savior's Lutheran Church in Colfax, North Dakota. In my mind I was throwing for my beloved Yankees in the World Series against the dastardly (Brooklyn) Dodgers or the beastly (Milwaukee) Braves.

I do know that my players enjoyed our visualization exercises. After the first few times the giggling subsided. Even when I introduced the flights-of-imagination style of visualizing, they kept their eyes closed and seemed to be experiencing what I was talking them through.

---

*John Gagliardi, St. John's (Minnesota) football coach, has his players routinely practice without contact to avoid injuries and ensure that his team is healthy for games. While most college and high school coaches are skeptical of this approach, Gagliardi has won more college football games than all but one other coach in history.

There is a great story about Phil Jackson's use of meditation with the Chicago Bulls. When Jackson first introduced the practice, Michael Jordan cracked open his eyes to see if his teammates were buying this strange idea. He discovered that they all seemed to be doing it (at least they had their eyes closed and were quiet). My players not only kept their eyes closed and were quiet, they began to tell me that they visualized in bed the night before a game, and I began to give each player an individual visualization exercise addressing an area of her game that needed improving.

In the early part of my second year of coaching, I was so focused on introducing a new offense and two new defensive systems to the team that I neglected visualization. Finally after a few weeks as we got close to our first game without having visualized, the players asked, "Are we going to do any visualization?" After that I made sure to save time at the end of practice at least two or three times a week for visualization.

Sports, above all else, are supposed to be fun. When we obsess on winning, or even on improving to our potential, we can forget how beautiful and joyful the activity itself is. Visualization can help us become re-enchanted with our game.

3. *Isolation and focus.* Another advantage of visualization is that it makes it easier to isolate the activity in question away from the distraction of opposing players, the roar of the crowd, and even the comments of your own coach and teammates. In *Positive Coaching*, I wrote about my experiences learning karate years ago. I had a karate teacher named Larry Sieberlich who knew enough to leave me alone for a while after he had shown me how to do something. He gave me the privacy to work out the mechanics without feeling that I was under his microscope all the time.

Visualization allows a player to focus all of her attention on what she is trying to do correctly. Then, when she has it mastered in her head, and then on the floor, she can let all the distractions back in and work on keeping focused in spite of them.

4. *Head starts.* There is no substitute for experience. Someone once said the greater part of courage comes from having done the thing

before. In the National Football League and the National Basketball Association, there's a widespread belief that it takes a year or more of knocking on the door of the Super Bowl or NBA Finals before a team can expect to win it all. There are just some intangible lessons that can only be learned by having been there.

You can't do something *before* you do it for the first time. However, visualization can *approximate* the experience before you do it for real. So, in a sense visualization *can* help you be there, or at least *feel* like you have been, before you get there. Worried about getting nervous when you go to the free throw line with the league title on the line? Pre-live the moment successfully again and again in your mind before you actually experience it for real.

5. *Enlisting the power of the imagination*. Perhaps the most important advantage of visualization is the impact it can have on the morale of people who are trying to change or bring about change. Einstein said "Imagination is more important than knowledge." Ideas have power, and captivating ideas further powered by our imagination can literally transform our lives. Imagination brings an awesome force into the situation.

Visualization can capture the imagination in a penetrating way and help align the internal forces needed to fuel the hard work of behavioral change. When you can see yourself succeeding over and over again in the privacy of your mind, it can provide a boost of emotional energy, and lots of emotional energy is needed to excel in any kind of competitive endeavor.

Would I recommend visualization to other coaches? That depends. It certainly isn't a quick fix. You still need to practice hard and do all the other things that make it possible to improve your performance. The key is the attitude of the coach. If a coach doesn't believe in it, he won't be able to sell his team on it. If a coach feels silly and unable to *act as if* he doesn't feel silly, then it is unlikely that the players will be able to take it seriously. Some coaches may just not believe visualization to be as valuable an activity as using that time for additional real-world practice or dispensing last-minute instructions in the locker room before the game.

It is also possible to use visualization effectively to reinforce the wrong thing. My friend Jo Felsenthal shared her ill-fated experience with visualization as a high school basketball player. Her coach had the team visualize being rooted in the ground like huge trees. When the game started, the players felt sluggish, just as if they were, indeed, rooted in place!

There are two possible scenarios that argue in favor of using visualization. The first is that more and more coaches will begin using the technique, leaving coaches that do not at a competitive disadvantage when their teams meet (assuming, as I do, that visualization is effective in improving performance). The other scenario is that not very many coaches will use it and the few who do can create a competitive advantage for themselves when their team plays those pedestrian "other" teams.

If a coach believes it can make a difference, finds it kind of funky and interesting to do, and is willing to prepare seriously for it the way he would prepare for any other aspect of coaching a sport, then I say go for it.

Journal Entry—July 5, 1996

I got so charged up I wrote an op-ed piece this weekend. I've been reading with amazement the articles and outraged letters to various editors about Hillary Clinton's imaginary conversations with Eleanor Roosevelt. Perhaps I've been living in Northern California too long, but what she's doing seems not only reasonable but also entirely healthy to me. Mrs. Clinton, like Mrs. Roosevelt, has been taking a battering from political enemies and pundits. Everything that could have gone wrong for her seems to, yet she is demonstrating the ability to persevere, even to the point of making a joke about checking with Mrs. Roosevelt at the beginning of a recent speech. What amazes me about this is that she is using catastrophization, a tool that many great athletes use to prepare themselves for competition. While Mrs. Clinton gets beat up about it, Dan O'Brien is applauded for using similar techniques to help himself recover from the devastating effects of not making the 1992 Olympics in the Decathlon when he failed to clear any height in the pole vault. I have been writing about visualization for the last few weeks and then this hits the news! I admire both Mrs. Clinton and Dan O'Brien for their mental toughness and just hope this whole media non-event helps bring the practice of visualization into more common usage among average people.

Take-Aways

Visualization and Transformation

1. Take stock of your own feelings toward using visualization. Do you have reservations about it? Do you fear that others will think you are strange or off-beat to try something like this? If you are tentative or uneasy about visualization, those feelings will come through to your players.

2. Become familiar with the different forms and mechanics of visualization
   a. Rehearsal of perfect performance, in which players visualize and "feel" themselves performing mechanical tasks such as shooting a free throw.
   b. Catastrophization, in which players are asked to visualize themselves persevering in spite of bad things happening.
   c. Flights of imagination, in which players imagine themselves as powerful animals or other forces of nature.

3. Prepare players for visualization by sharing with them stories of famous athletes who have used visualization successfully. Try to use athletes that they are familiar with and admire. If possible, have a successful person who uses visualization come to practice to talk with players about it.

4. When you introduce visualization to your players, expect some resistance and even embarrassment from them. It is natural for players to feel funny about a new technique that they are being exposed to for the first time. Ask them if the are willing to try to work through the discomfort and give it a try.

5. Develop an outline of what you want to say for your first few visualizations with your team. If you don't feel comfortable working from an outline, write out a script and read it verbatim. Either way, don't rush it. Give the players time to see and feel what you are describing.

6. Introduce players to vizualization involving both an internal camera, in which they see the court as if through their own eyes, and an external camera, in which they see themselves on the court as if on a videotape. Encourage them to become comfortable with both kinds.

7. Encourage players to do visualization in bed before they go to sleep. Give them individual visualization assignments tied to skills they need to master.

8. Experiment with visualization yourself. Write down the elements of a perfect coaching performance as you see them. Visualize yourself coaching the perfect game according to those elements.

Chapter 8

Rookie Moves and Tough Calls: Reflections on Coachly Decision Making

. . . An organization facing competition is likely to respond . . . through a localized search and decision process. This response then marginally increases the competition faced by the organization's rivals, triggering in them a similar process of search and decision—which ultimately increases the competitive pressures faced by the first organization. This again triggers the search for improvements in the first organization, and so the cycle continues.

—William P. Barnett and Morten T. Hansen,
The Red Queen in Organizational Evolution

The Thickness of the Air

There once was a major-league baseball scout who begins to hear tales about a young pitching phenom from a rural community who, legend has it, can throw smoke. This is long before the advent of radar guns and video cameras so there is only one way for him to verify the fastball of this young farm boy. The scout makes the long train ride to a small city, in which he catches the bus for an additional extended ride to a tiny town, in which he hires a horse to ride out to the junction where the hired man is waiting to take him to the boy's farm. Being a grizzled and skeptical scout, he is prepared to be disappointed. However, when he sees the strapping youngster's delivery and hears the hum of his nearly invisible fastball out behind the barn where the youngster's father had built a pitching mound for him, he began to feel just the slightest bit of excitement tingle down his spine. No other scout has been willing to make the considerable effort to visit this boy and he begins to imagine the stories that will one day be told about how he discovered the next Bob ("Rapid Robert") Feller.

He signs the boy to a contract and within a few weeks has him pitching in the major leagues. There is only one problem with the boy's debut performance: The heretofore invisible fast ball is highly visible to the batters and becomes invisible only after disappearing, repeatedly, over the outfield fence.

As the scout is putting the young man on the bus back home, he just has to know what went wrong. He asks the young man what happened to his fast ball, to which the youth replies "The air ain't so thick back behind the barn."

As one moves from being an interested observer in the bleachers to being the decision maker on the sidelines, one becomes aware of the complexity of trying to coach a simple game like basketball. Does the air thicken on the court during the heat of a closely contested contest? Is that why decisions that seem so easy from the vantage point of the stands, or the easy chair in front of the television, become so perplexing?

This chapter is about coachly decision making and some reflections that have occurred to me over the past two years. In particular I want to focus on three general difficulties that coaches face.

The first is the Rookie Move, the mistake that in retrospect seems so obvious you are embarrassed when you think about it. Then there are the kinds of coaching decisions that will always be difficult because of the so-called Red Queen Effect, the fact that sports involve competitive contests between two teams and sets of coaches that are trying and thinking as hard as they can about how to defeat the other team. These are the Tough Calls and, while experience may give you some rules of thumb, tough calls will always be tough to call. Finally, I will return to the initial question: How does one deal with the fact that performance degrades in the "thick air" of competition?

Let's start with the first hurdle a new coach faces, the tendency to make Rookie Moves.

Rookie Moves

Years ago in St. Paul, Minnesota, my friend Pete was driving a car carrying my friend Susan and me. He moved to the lefthand lane and had to sit for several minutes while the car ahead of him tried in vain to make a left turn during rush hour. Pete, after waiting patiently for a couple of minutes, suddenly shouted at himself in frustration "Rookie move!"

Pete and I lost track of each other over the years, but his legacy lingered. From then on, whenever Susan ended up stuck behind some driver trying to turn left in the face of oncoming traffic, she referred to Pete's epithet. And to this day more than 20 years later, I never fail to hear Pete yelling "Rookie move!" whenever I warily switch to the lefthand lane.

Rookie Moves are mistakes that people new to a profession or activity make simply because they haven't been confronted with them before, the kinds of mistakes one rarely makes after getting some experience. One of the most traumatic Rookie Moves I made as a coach had to do with substitutions.

Journal Entry—November 26, 1995

Yesterday, after our scrimmage with Woodside, one of the players asked if she could talk to me. I took her aside and she started crying. It turned out she was upset that she hadn't gotten to play as much as she would have liked in the scrimmage. I explained to her that with our first game looming, I felt the need to let the starters play together as much as possible so they would be ready for Monday's game.

She said she felt that I only focused on the top five players and ignored the rest of the team. I disagreed only in her estimation of the number. I told her that I did indeed focus more attention on the top seven players and that right now she was the number 10 player and that she would need to come to practice regularly and work harder if she were going to see more playing time. She didn't like this at all and left still crying.

I felt terrible. I told Miguel about this and asked him what he thought. He has been coaching at the high school level much longer than I have. He said he would have told her "You think I'm focusing on the top five? You're right. What you need to do is get to be one of the top five! Until then, stop complaining."

I'm ambivalent. I'm glad that I was honest with her. But I also felt that I was a little harder-edged than I needed to be in telling her where she stood in terms of playing time. I think I felt attacked by her and I responded less kindly than I wish I had.

Substitutions and Valuing Players

In *Dorothy Day: A Radical Devotion*, Robert Coles' biography of the founder of the Catholic Worker movement, Coles describes his first meeting with the saintly Ms. Day.

> "She was sitting at a table, talking with a woman who was, I quickly realized, quite drunk, yet determined to carry on a conversation . . . The woman . . . had a large purple-red birthmark along the right side of her forehead. She kept touching it as she uttered one exclamatory remark after another, none of which seemed to get the slightest rise from the person sitting opposite her.
>
> I found myself increasingly confused by what seemed to be an interminable, essentially absurd exchange taking place between the two middle-aged women. When would it end—the alcoholic ranting and the silent nodding, occasionally interrupted by a brief question, which only served, maddeningly, to wind up the already overtalkative one rather than wind her down? Finally, silence fell upon the room. Dorothy Day asked the woman if she would mind an interruption. She got up and came over to me. She said, 'Are you waiting to talk with one of us?'"

Coles was impressed with Day's humility, given that she was a writer and a person of intellect while her partner in conversation was a mentally ill woman. It would have been natural for the reknowned Dorothy Day to assume that someone hovering around would have been there to speak to her. Coles again:

> "*One of us*: with those three words she had cut through layers of self-importance, a lifetime of bourgeois privilege, and scraped the hard bone of pride: 'Vanity of vanities; all is vanity.'"

For some reason, this story comes to mind when I think about substitutions in basketball games. I believe coaches too easily slip into valuing players in proportion to how much they can help them win games, and I didn't want that to happen to me. At some level, I think I want to be like Dorothy Day, who equally valued homeless, mentally ill alcoholics and bright, college-educated intellectuals like Robert Coles. I also want to be able to value each person regardless of how talented or articulate or rich or powerful. As a coach, I wanted to value each player regardless of what she could do on the basketball court. Somehow this got scrambled in my mind, so that valuing players became roughly equated with how playing time was allocated among them.

This kind of muddled thinking set up a conflict in my head between "saintliness" and having a winning record, and led to a continuing struggle to balance the needs of the team with that of the individual players. In high school basketball this usually comes down to playing time. Few players ever feel they get enough playing time. As a coach, I wanted to win as many games as possible *and* give everyone enough playing time to satisfy them. This, I quickly learned, was impossible. Some players with limited skills may be more than happy to get in a game here or there for a minute or two each time. But others with equally limited skills see themselves to be much more talented than the coach does. They aren't happy playing the limited but critical role of preparing the starters for the next game. They want to be a starter and believe, against all the physical evidence, that they are equal to or better than the starters.

I had coached in a number of situations with younger players before coaching at the high school level. In almost every situation, there were league rules that forced coaches to play all their players, if not equally, at least equitably. But I didn't need the rules. I was enthusiastic about playing everyone and even convinced myself that it had a team-building benefit that more than made up for any poor play the less-talented players engaged in on the floor. Subconsciously, I may have assumed that I would be a rare, saint-like coach who played everyone and still won! I was setting myself up for a big fall and it didn't take long to come.

It came during an early-season game in my first year, when I substituted one of my weaker players during the last minute or so of the first half of a tight game. This player had been bugging me about increased playing time for some time. I thought "What can happen in 30 seconds?" I soon found out.

She went into the game without finding out who she was supposed to guard. Her opposite number quickly realized she was unmarked and immediately cut to the basket, where she found a pass waiting for an easy lay-up. On the next play my substitute got the ball out beyond the three-point line and immediately shot an air ball. The opposing center gathered in the short shot and threw a baseball pass the length of the floor to her point guard, who scored as the first-half buzzer sounded. We never recovered and what had been a potential nail-biter became a character-building game of a different sort for me.

Following this painful experience, I worked hard to develop an intellectual understanding and rationale for how to balance the trade-off between substituting liberally versus trying to win as many games as possible. Here's what I came up with.

First, I found I could not continue to live in a dream world. If we were going to win many games, I needed to have my best players on the court most of the time. In sorting through this realization, I also realized that playing time didn't need to serve as a proxy for how much I valued each player. I could be as committed to the least-talented player as the star scorer without giving them equal playing time. After all, one of the primary gifts Dorothy Day gave the mentally ill woman described by Robert Coles was the gift of listening to her. Why did I assume that "Coach Day," after listening patiently and caringly to her player complain about lack of playing time, would have put her into a game during crunch time?

I came to see that at the high school level, you are coaching players of varying levels of both ability and commitment. Many of my players had made huge commitments to the team and the sport. They attended summer camps, participated in off-season workouts, lifted weights, played in spring and summer leagues, and came to practice every day ready to give it their all.

Not all players make that kind of commitment. Often the players who complain the loudest about lack of playing time are the very ones who miss one or more practices each week. By treating all players "equally" in terms of playing time, I was actually undermining those who had made the kind of commitment I encouraged them to make. Neither saint-like nor smart!

Journal Entry—March 10, 1996

Yesterday was the end-of-the-year Jamboree for Cupertino Hoops and the first ever ceremony for the Jason Owings Positive Coaching Awards.

Last June I got a call from Sandy Owings Dumont, the mother of Jason Owings, a young man who had coached for two years with Cupertino Hoops. I was distressed to hear that Jason had drowned in a swimming accident in the Yuba River in northern California, just a few weeks shy of his 23rd birthday.

Sandy told me how much Jason had loved basketball and coaching in Cupertino Hoops. The family had decided that they would ask mourners to give money to Cupertino Hoops rather than buy flowers. Would the league be interested in (and able to use productively) those donations? I was thinking in terms of a couple of hundred dollars and told her that we would be honored to apply the funds to scholarships for youth who couldn't afford the league fee.

As more than $10,000 rolled in—Mike Owings, Jason's father, worked in the sporting apparel industry and had called on some of his contacts for large donations—I realized that we needed to figure out something else to do with the money because we didn't have *that* many kids needing scholarships. One of the recommendations from the Communitarian Network's Building Character Through Sports Task Force of which I am a member is to create awards at all levels of sports for coaches who build character in their athletes. In most youth sports leagues, the positive reinforcement goes to the coaches who win. They are the ones in Little League who get to coach the all-star team that continues playing after the regular season is over. Why not use some of the Owings Fund to create an award to recognize positive coaches?

Yesterday, with all of Jason's family and many of his friends in attendance, we awarded five Jason Owings Awards. After announcing the names of Scott Farrell, Darrell Kettner, Sheldon Orton, and Robert Williams, I paused to relish what was to come next.

Mike Bright was the last person to win an award. Because he is a board member, initially he was considered ineligible. The board decided last fall that board members were ineligible for the award, at least in the first year. Mike and Ron Rossi and I met to review the nominations submitted by parents, players, and fellow coaches. Mike coached two teams this year and got a ton of nominations from both parents and players. But since he wasn't eligible, we didn't even look at those nominations. After I got home I read through them and practically cried, they were so heartfelt. I realized that we simply couldn't not give the award to Mike, that it wouldn't be fair to penalize him just because he was a board member. I called the rest of the selection committee and the board chairs and they all agreed that Mike should get the award. That next week I got another nomination by fax from Jamie, an athlete with Down syndrome who played on one of Mike's teams.

In announcing the first four winners, I read some of the things that had been written about each by the parents, players, and other coaches who had nominated them. Then I announced that we had a special winner, one that we simply couldn't turn down even though he was a board member, and asked Mike to come forward to get his award. Immediately, about 30 people in the stands started clapping and cheering and stomping their feet. It turns out a lot of Mike's players and parents had been quite upset when they were told that Mike was ineligible for the award, so when they heard he was getting it they went nuts.

When I started reading what parents and players had said about Mike, I mentioned that one of Mike's players had faxed me a nomination. I mentioned Jamie's name and said he had written some touching things about how Mike had helped him enjoy and become better at basketball. As I started to read Jamie's statement, he came down from the stands and ran over and gave Mike a big hug. I hope someone got a picture of that. Moments like that are why I coach basketball!

The Preciousness of Momentum

Another blinding insight that was not obvious to me as a rookie coach revolved around the importance of momentum. **Momentum** is **huge.** More than that, it is **humongous!** It is incredibly important, not just in sports, but also in life.

The difference between having momentum on your side and having it against you is the difference between running uphill and running downhill. We wouldn't expect someone running uphill to be able to beat a closely matched runner who was allowed to run downhill. Momentum causes many people, in fact, to walk down a flight of stairs but take the elevator up. **Momentum is huge** (I know I am repeating myself, but *I am on a roll!*). I can see that oh-so-clearly now, but it took a costly incidence in which I squandered precious momentum to bring the lesson home to me.

In a mid-season game during my first season, we experienced a spurt of scoring and pulled out to a comfortable lead early in the game. The opposing coach substituted a couple of his starters and I thought to take advantage of that by giving some of my starters a rest, sending in four subs at once. This had two consequences that still cause me to cringe even as I write this. First, I disrupted the flow of momentum that my team was enjoying. As Phil Kelly, the athletic director, told me afterward while I figuratively sobbed on his shoulder, "Momentum is a precious thing." You don't want to squander momentum when you stumble onto it as I had done. By the time I got my starters back into the game, they were cold and had lost their earlier flow.

The second problem was that I had left no one on the floor capable of guarding the other team's point guard. The rest of her supporting cast was not stellar but she quickly recognized that she was no longer being covered like a glove and proceeded to drive for three baskets in a row. On her last drive she was fouled and made the free throw as well! This stopped the clock, which allowed me to get my starters back in the game, but our comfortable lead had shrunk to nothing. We ended up losing the game by a basket when a department-store mannequin as coach would have won it! In our post-game talk, I apologized to the players for having lost the game with my coaching decisions.

Insult was added to injury when one of the parents, a person who had been very supportive of me up to that point, approached me as I headed out the gymnasium door. Totally abject about the debacle, I began to apologize once again, but was greeted with a frigid blast of negativity before I could say anything. Later Lori, my assistant coach, told me she thought the parent was really out of line, but I was torn. I tended to agree with the parent, even as I was hurt and angry about what felt like a personal attack. I realized then, if I hadn't known it before, that parents of players aren't necessarily the place for a coach to go for moral support when he does something stupid.

I remember a conversation I had with a coach a few weeks after we had beaten his team. He said his players' parents got down on him because they thought he had "given up" on his players too soon. I had substituted freely when we got up by fifteen points early in the third quarter, and he followed suit. His parents had wanted him to keep the starters in. He told them that he appreciated my not trying to run up the score, that if he had kept his starters in and gotten the score close, I would simply have put my starters back in. One of his parents said "He can do that?" The coach said that was when he realized that this was a conversation that wasn't going anywhere he wanted to be.

One reason Rookie Moves are so prevalent with rookies is that new coaches are so consumed with the quotidian demands of the job. There is so much "stuff" to worry about (keeping track of the basketballs, making sure the bleachers get pulled out, who'll be the scorekeeper tonight, who'll run the time clock, who'll keep the stats, etc., etc., etc.). Over time you get policies, procedures, and people in place so that you can focus more of your creative energy on the actual coaching. But that usually takes time.

Someone once said that anyone can learn from their own mistakes, whereas smart people learn from the mistakes of others. Rookie Moves can certainly be minimized by learning from other people's mistakes or from apprenticing with a master. But even then there simply isn't any way to do something before you do it the first time. Rookie Moves are inevitable. You simply have to experience them and then you won't make the same mistake again.

The Tough Calls

So far we've looked at errors of inexperience. If Rookie Moves were the only problem for a coach, then all you'd have to do to become a great coach is to endure. Just hang around until you get lots of experience and you automatically get better and better!

But some decisions don't lend themselves to the wisdom of experience. These are what I call the Tough Calls, the decisions that will always be difficult no matter how long you coach. Much of the difficulty has to do with the competitive nature of coaching.

The Red Queen

A big reason why coaching is so difficult is that you have an adversary who is trying to outwit you.* While you and your team are trying to do the best you can, you have an opponent who is trying his or her best to keep you from doing your best. You may have seen the bumper sticker "Even paranoids have enemies." Well, if you are a basketball coach, you don't need to wonder about paranoia. People really *are* out to get you!

This requires you to get better or fall behind. This has come to be called the Red Queen Effect after a memorable exchange between the Red Queen and Alice in Lewis Carroll's *Through the Looking-Glass*. It occurs immediately after Alice has run as fast as she can until she was out of breath:

> Alice looked around her in great surprise. "Why, I do believe we've been under this tree the whole time! Everything's just as it was!"
>
> "Of course it is," said the Queen. "What would you have it?"
>
> Well, in *our* country," said Alice, still panting a little, "you'd generally get to somewhere else—if you ran very fast for a long time as we've been doing."
>
> "A slow sort of country!" said the Queen. "Now, *here*, you see, it takes all the running *you* can do, to keep in the same place. If you want to get somewhere else, you must run at least twice as fast as that!"

In January 1997, Ben Braun, head coach of the University of California men's basketball team, tried a new strategy to deal with Brevin Knight, Stanford's All American point guard. He double-teamed Knight every time he touched the ball. It worked well, better than anything else had worked that year against Knight. It lead to a Cal victory over Stanford, and in the next two Stanford games Knight was again double-teamed. After that no other team double-teamed Brevin Knight for the rest of the season, not even Cal the second time they played. Why?

---

*For the sake of this discussion I am oversimplifying the contest as one between two coaches, which is wildly inaccurate given that players on both teams make decisions affecting the outcome.

The answer is that double-teaming Knight was no longer an advantageous tactic for opposing teams because Stanford's coach Mike Montgomery and Knight had learned how to adjust to it and they began to exploit it.

Notice that the Cal Bears had improved and, for a moment, had benefited from that tactical improvement. But Stanford then improved in response, and at the end of the three weeks both teams were better, but not better off. They were back to where they had started in terms of strength relative to each other, even though both were better teams than they had been three weeks before. In effect, they both were running faster just to stay in the same place.

There is a scene in the movie *Patton* that captures the essence of the problem for a coach. General Patton (played by George C. Scott) has just defeated the brilliant German Field Marshall Rommel in a tank battle. As Patton savors his victory from a nearby hill, he says rhetorically "Rommel, I read your book!" As crafty as Rommel was, he became more predictable after he wrote a book about his tactics. By learning Rommel's tendencies, Patton was able to anticipate and outwit him. By not considering that Patton would try to understand his tendencies, Rommel allowed himself to become predictable.

I remember the last few seconds of two games late in my first year at Fremont. Against Sacred Heart Cathedral in the CCS quarterfinals, we had the ball at midcourt on the far sidelines trailing by one basket with just enough time to get off one good shot. I used our last timeout to set up a play designed to get us that shot. What I failed to do was anticipate that our opponents might try to disrupt us. Instead of politely allowing us to inbounds the ball and run our play, they contested the inbounds pass aggressively. We weren't prepared for that and a SHC player intercepted the pass. I kicked myself for not anticipating this, especially since we had won a game a few weeks earlier when I correctly anticipated the reaction of the other team. In that situation, it was clear the other team would have to contest the inbounds pass because we had the ball and were ahead by two with fifteen seconds remaining. I instructed Jenny to fake toward our opponent's basket (the "logical" place to go) and then streak up court toward our basket. She looked at me as if I were crazy, but did as I asked. Her feint left her wide open and she went the length of the floor for an uncontested lay-up at the buzzer. The other team, expecting us to play conservatively with a slim lead, was unprepared for Jenny's aggressive move. I enjoyed her stunned look as she expressed her amazement that my weird idea had worked.

Journal Entry—Wednesday, January 16, 1995

What a mess! Saturday night Homestead played at Cupertino. I asked Jeff Myers, who had been filming many of our games for me, if he could videotape the game. He was busy, but offered to lend me his camera. I set myself up at the top of the bleachers opposite the scorer's table and videotaped the first half—fat, dumb and happy. At half-time the camera needed a charge, so I looked around for an outlet. At that point, Ernie walked over from where he was talking to his team to tell me he thought what I was doing was illegal—that it was league rules you could only videotape your own games. I told him I'd never heard of that and he said that he'd been out of the league for a few years, so maybe it wasn't a rule anymore, but it was at least a gentleman's agreement. I went ahead and videotaped the second half but decided I wouldn't look at the tape if I found out Ernie was right. I called Phil but he was out so I called Dave Crawford, who said he had never heard of anything like that, so I thought maybe Ernie was playing a mind-game with me. Late Sunday night I still hadn't heard from Phil and I was running out of time to watch the tape, so I did.

Monday morning I got a call from Phil. His phone had been ringing off the hook from the league and Ernie and the athletic director at Cupertino complaining about my violation of the videotaping rule. Yes, alas, it is a rule—it's just that I had never seen a copy of the by-laws. Phil assured me I was given them, but I have no clue where they are. Phil suggested I call Ernie and Debbie and apologize. I did, and they were both pretty good about it. I called Phil back to relate my conversations and he said the issue was over, that we wouldn't have to forfeit or anything. But I was embarrassed. Here I am a rookie coach and already it looks like I would do anything to win, including break the rules! Yikes!

Rich Kelley used to tell me that I didn't really understand the obsession that many coaches had about basketball, that they would spend hours reviewing videotape over and over looking for the slightest edge over their competition. Well, I guess I understand it only too well now. In fact, you might say that I have seen the obsessive coach and he is me.

So let's explore why the Red Queen makes it so hard to make the correct coaching decision in any given situation. Let's divide the world into a vastly simplified set of "naive" coaches and "crafty" coaches. Some coaches simply (and naively) focus on trying to play their game. Craftier coaches also concern themselves with disrupting their opponents' best-laid plans. As a would-be crafty coach, you have two responsibilities: (1) to develop your game plan for how you want to play; and (2) to anticipate what your opponent is going to do and figure out how to disrupt that.

It gets more complicated if you also are competing against a crafty coach. Let's assume that you know your opponent to be crafty. In this case you can assume that she will be trying to anticipate and disrupt you. In this case, you not only need (1) to develop your game plan, and (2) how you intend to disrupt her, you also need (3) to anticipate how she will try to disrupt you, and (4) plan for that.

But in the real world, there are many more than two categories. In addition to always-naive and always-crafty coaches, there are also the sometimes-crafty-sometimes-naive coaches. Even crafty coaches make anticipatory blunders, and every once in awhile naive coaches stumble onto a brilliant anticipatory stratagem.

Furthermore, until you've been around a while you may not know whether a particular coach is naive or crafty. Some coaches are constant learners so they may start out being naive but become more and more crafty each year. If you don't know where they are on their craftiness evolutionary curve, you can misjudge them badly. You can outguess yourself when you believe you know that your opponent is anticipating you but he really isn't! And what if he is crafty but believes you also to be crafty so he acts naive so as to confound you who expect him to be crafty?

If this isn't complicated enough, there is another source of uncertainty to drive coaches crazy. This is due to the difference between planning and implementation.

Let's say you are playing a team with a really shrewd, crafty coach. She is able to develop wonderful game plans but just doesn't have the talent to carry them out. Do you plan for a crafty coach or a naive one? The best ideas can look like failures due to poor implementation.

I remember reading David Levine's *Life on the Rim*, about the Continental Basketball Association, featuring George Karl, coach of the

Albany Patroons, later to coach the Seattle Supersonics in the NBA. Again and again, in last-second pressure situations, Karl designed plays that got his shooters open for good looks at the basket. Almost always they missed! He was smart enough always to get them a good shot, but as smart as he was he couldn't make the ball go in the basket.

I tried and tried to get my players to use a trick out-of-bounds play that my team had used successfully when I played high school basketball in West Fargo, North Dakota. The play can only be used when you are taking the ball out of bounds under your own basket. One player takes the ball from the referee and then another player saunters up saying loudly, "Wait, *I'm* supposed to take it out!" The player with the ball tosses a legal pass to the shouting player, who just happens to be standing under the basket. The shouter becomes a shooter and scores while the astonished opposing team tries to figure out what just happened. We practiced it several times in practice but we just couldn't pull it off in a game. Perhaps my players were just too straightforward and honest!

On the other hand, a truly naive coach can have subpar ideas that look brilliant if he has talented, committed people figuring out how to make them work. I remember reading about how smart everyone thought Paul Brown was when he coached the Cleveland Browns in the 1950s. After Otto Graham, his star quarterback, retired, he didn't seem so smart. Later, revisionist sports historians attributed a great deal of Coach Brown's success to having a really crafty quarterback running his offense.

To summarize, as a would-be crafty coach you need to worry about the following variables:

- Whether the opposing coach is naive or crafty (or sometimes one and sometimes the other);

- Whether you have perfect information about his naiveté or craftiness;

- Whether this naive coach is acting craftily in this case (or vice versa);

- Whether your crafty opponent sees you as crafty, in which case she may try to out-think you, perhaps by being especially crafty by acting naive;

- Whether your crafty opponent has the talent to implement his crafty ideas;

- Whether your naive opponent has a crafty athlete or two who implement her naive ideas with a crafty flair; and

- Whether you are in danger of outguessing yourself by trying to anticipate everything that your opponent might do, including correctly anticipating what *you* intend to do, and then anticipating *his* anticipations, and on and on and on like the "Sunny Jim" peanut butter jar label with a picture of a boy holding a jar of peanut butter with a label with a picture of a boy holding a jar of peanut butter with a label . . .

The last danger is portrayed in *The Princess Bride*, a hysterical movie and an even better book—by William Goldman. The hero and the villain have decided to compete in a duel to the death using their wits rather than brawn. They are about to choose goblets of wine to drink, one of which apparently has been laced with poison by the hero. The villain, played by Wallace Shawn, tries to anticipate which goblet the hero would have poisoned. After several iterations of his thought process, the villain chooses one of the goblets, certain that he has outguessed the hero. The hero drinks the other and then . . . the villain drops dead. When asked how he could so confidently know which goblet the villain would choose, the hero reveals that they *both* were poisoned! He had anticipated this moment and had been gradually taking increasing bits of poison over time until he had built up an immunity to it! (Kids, don't try this at home!)

And, of course, this model is still much simpler than real life, which has many other variables that we haven't even discussed. For example, is your coaching opponent "smart" or "dull"? Just because someone is crafty doesn't mean she will be smart about her craftiness. And what about innovation? An opposing coach could be either an innovator, someone who is likely to try new approaches, or a "traditionalist" who uses the same offensive and defensive sets year after year without fail, perhaps because they once worked well. Then there is flexibility. Some coaches vary their strategy and tactics to reflect the strengths and weaknesses of their players. Others are rigid and insist on a pre-set method of play without regard for the characteristics of their players. I could go on, but I won't!

This incredible complexity about what most people probably see as a fairly simple game, leads many coaches to throw up their hands at anything but the simplest kind of anticipatory gamesmanship, and to focus primarily or solely on trying to play their own game without reference to the opposition. Discouraged by what Von Clausewitz called "the fog of war," they give up trying to become a truly crafty coach.

Rough Magic, Lowell Cohn's book about Bill Walsh's return to coach the Stanford Football team, discusses the advantage Stanford had over Penn State in the Blockbuster Bowl on January 1, 1993. "To (assistant coach Scott) Schuhmann, Paterno was a good coach who cared about his players and, like Walsh, had all the right priorities when it came to university life, but no one ever would compare Paterno to Walsh as a tactician. Give Walsh extra time to prepare for an opponent—in this case almost a month—and he was unbeatable. He'd already proven that with three Super Bowl victories and two bowl wins in his previous tenure at Stanford." After spending considerable time examining film of Penn State's earlier games, Stanford won the Blockbuster Bowl 24-3.

So, as difficult as it is to become a crafty coach, to anticipate your opponent's moves and his countermoves of his anticipated idea of your moves, it is the key to moving up to the next level of coaching.

Imperfect Information Problems

Other tough calls can result because of imperfect information about your opponent.

Solving the Wrong Problem

At the end of the 1996 season, we ended up scheduled to play our opening-round CCS game against North Salinas High School at their gym. This was an improvement from the year before, when we had to travel an hour further to get to King City, a city so far south I couldn't believe it was in the *Central* Coast Section. However, North Salinas had a 22-4 record and we had not played anyone who had played them, to be able to get a reliable scouting report.

I did get a moment at the CCS seeding meeting to talk with Ken Kline, the King City coach, whose team had lost by seven points to North

Salinas in an early season game. He stressed the quickness of their guards and how well they applied pressure. He also told me that we would have little trouble inside against their big girls, who were young. He well remembered that Colleen had scored 30 points against King City in CCS the previous year.

We spent our few days of practice before the North Salinas game preparing to deal with pressure. We went five against seven with the extra two defenders being free to double team anyone at any time. We worked on having our guards make passes before a double team could reach them. By the time of our game with North Salinas, I was not worried about their pressure. I also wasn't worried about their inside game.

Although the North Salinas guards were indeed quick, we were well prepared and had few turnovers. But the game was decided, as it often is, by rebounding. We were out-rebounded badly, completely losing the war on the boards. The North Salinas Vikings—a mismatch of community and team mascot comparable to the Utah Jazz—were a ferocious bunch of rebounders, and they were significantly more muscular than our girls. It is rare to win a basketball game when you are badly out-rebounded and we didn't buck the odds in this case.

And, if imperfect information about your opponent is a common problem, sometimes you don't even have good information about your own team!

Firing Up vs. Calming Down

There was another reason we lost the North Salinas game. We missed a lot of easy shots. That is in part because we prepared for a different team than the one we played. We played a big, muscular team that banged us around. It's harder than you'd think to make a two-foot shot when you've been bumped and banged on previous shot attempts. But we also missed easy shots because I had misread the state of mind of my players. I had cranked them up when they already were nervous about the game and needed to be calmed down.

In retrospect, I can see that the seniors were not relaxed. The year before, as juniors, they had been calm going into the playoffs, probably feeling they didn't have too much to lose since they would be back the next year. We did as well as we did then largely because of the contributions of the juniors with Colleen, Jenny, and Haruka all playing better than they had all year. This time around, I believe they felt the weight of the "last game." They didn't want their high school careers ending just yet and they were playing *not to lose* rather than to win. But I simply didn't see that.

At various times during the season I could tell when the team was at low energy. Sometimes I would even ask some of the players if they thought the team needed to get fired up. Other times I could tell they were nervous and I geared my pre-game talk and visualization exercise to calm them down. But sometimes the players themselves can't tell you what they need, or you read the signs the wrong way and make the wrong call.

This is why the choice between firing-them-up or calming-them-down is a Tough Call. Certainly experience helps, but sometimes you are going to make the wrong call regardless of how long you have been coaching.

Sometimes You Lose No Matter What

There is another reality and that is that sometimes you can do all your coachly things perfectly and you will still lose. Sometimes you simply come up against a better team, and you lose. After I saw North Salinas play two more games—they defeated a powerful St. Francis team and were finally eliminated by Homestead, the ultimate Division II CCS Champion in a close game—I concluded that they hadn't gotten a 22-4 regular season record simply because they were lucky or had played only inferior teams.

Thick Air Revisited

One reason why coaching is a difficult thing to do well is that many coaching decisions must be made in the heat of battle, in the moment, in "real time" as they say in the computer industry. Blunders that you just wouldn't make if you had the time to reflect, to consult with others, to sleep on it overnight, pop out of your mouth with regularity when you are pressed for time. This is due, in part, to the Thick Air Effect described at the beginning of this chapter.

There is a lot at stake in coaching, even though "it's just a game." The fact that it is just a game with no inherent meaning doesn't help much. So what if no one is going to die if you lose a game? It feels that important. The fact that so many people are so passionate about a game like high school basketball is a good example of the concept of "socially constructed reality." In other words, it's only important because a lot of people, as part of the culture, treat it as if it is important. But the reality is that socially constructed reality is real! As I write this, I note that I have ten unchewed fingernails, something that *never* occurs during a basketball season when I am coaching.

The best advice I've run across to deal with the Thick Air problem came from my colleague Alison Carlson, who told me what Billie Jean King says about pressure: "Pressure is a privilege." Very few people get the chance to perform in front of an audience that cares passionately about the outcome, that cares enough to pay for a ticket to be there. Those who do are privileged, and the price one pays for that privilege is chewed fingernails or the equivalent. When I think of it that way, I can almost (almost!) feel pleasure in being in the spotlight, having to make an on-the-spot decision that will determine the outcome of the game. And I know that I have been, at least for a while, among the privileged.

Take-Aways

Rookie Moves and Tough Calls

1. Recognize that Rookie Moves are inevitable and give yourself some slack. Learn to forgive yourself when you make a Rookie Move. Learn from it but then move on to the next challenge. An advanced approach for dealing with Rookie Moves is to learn to laugh at them. Trust me, this gets easier as time passes.

2. Work on getting people and procedures in place to deal with as many of the administrative details as possible so you can focus your creative energy on the strategic aspects of coaching.

3. Find ways to express your valuing of your players that aren't tied to how much playing time you allocate to them.

4. Appreciate the gift of momentum. Try not to screw it up when it comes your way!

5. Embrace the Red Queen. See the necessity to get better just to stay in the same place as a challenge rather than a burden.

6. Decide whether you want to become a crafty coach. Recognize the hard mental work involved in doing so. If you do, then
   a. Learn as much as you can about the coaches and teams that you will be playing. Develop a game plan that will give you a chance of disrupting what they like to do.
   b. When playing against a team coached by a crafty coach, as part of your game plan think about your and your team's tendencies. Imagine what you would do to disrupt *your* team if you were the opposing coach. Develop a plan for responding to the other team's disruptions.
   c. Don't overdo it. Beware of spending so much time trying to anticipate your opponent's moves that you forget to allocate enough thinking and practice time to developing your own.

7. Remember that sometimes you lose no matter what you do. Use losses to learn how to do a better job next time, rather than to beat yourself over the head.

8. Recognize how lucky you are to be coaching a team in a competitive situation. Relish the challenge of putting forth your best effort. Remember that pressure is a privilege. Enjoy your privileged position.

Abrupt Ending #2

Death, thou comest when I had thee least in mind.
— Peter Mathiesson, **Far Tortuga**

Journal Entry — Thursday, May 22, 1996

Yesterday afternoon I worked out at the YMCA. As I checked out, the
young woman behind the desk asked me about the CCS (Central Coast
Section) T-shirt I was wearing. "What sport is your CCS shirt from?"
"Basketball," I told her. "I'm the varsity girls basketball coach at
Fremont High School in Sunnyvale."

It turned out that she had participated in the CCS track tournament
for Westmont High. For some reason this conversation made me
happy. As I began to jog the half-mile home I had an energy in my step
inconsistent with the fact that I had already run six and a half miles. I
realized that I was happy because I was proud of being the Fremont
High School girls basketball coach and very much looking forward to
the next season.

This is a surprise of sorts because even though I had decided to coach again I have been feeling burned out for some time. The season, although it had ended on an incredible upper with the streak and the league title, had been a hard one for me. But I knew things were turning around psychologically and that I was getting my emotional energy back, because I had recently ordered a coaching video on a high post offense designed for teams that lack a dominant center. I had already spent several hours studying it and designing plays. I had begun imagining what it would be like to have a team with as much speed as we would have with Natalie and Chi being joined by Beatrice, Sarah, Charlotte, Keri, and the others up from the JV team next year. We'll be small but we'll be faster than the past two years. Our scramble defense could be even more strangulating than this year. As the sign says "Speed Kills!" In fact, that would make a cool T-shirt for the next generation of WWF.

Until this point I hadn't realized how excited I am about next season.

Journal Entry — Friday, May 23, 1996

What can I say? Yesterday I finally got over to Fremont to inventory the uniforms. Phil had been leaving me increasingly irritated phone messages for several weeks about getting that done. But the combination of moving into a new house, traveling to Brazil with a group of MBA students, going back to North Dakota for my mother's heart surgery, and a lot of things going on at work, I just hadn't been able to get over there. Part of it also was undoubtedly that I didn't enjoy doing inventory. I remember when I was a counselor at Camp Owendigo in Minnesota years ago, my performance evaluation was tops in every category except one. My boss, Betsy Lightbourn, wrote "Jim could take better care of the supplies."

Pat (the other athletic director) came over as I was doing the inventory. She told me she needed the points for my players to determine who would get varsity letters. She asked me to wait until she returned with the forms before I left. She was emphatic. "Make sure you don't leave before I come back." No problem.

I went through the mail that had accumulated in the girls basketball box while I waited. When she finally returned, she asked the only student in the room if he would excuse himself for a while. I still wasn't picking up the signals. It wasn't until she pulled up a chair that I began to realize that something was up.

"You know that the teacher's union has a contract provision that an on-campus teacher can claim any extracurriculur activity that's handled by an off-campus coach." Well, actually, no, I didn't know that.

So, abruptly my coaching career at Fremont High School ends.

As with most things, I have mixed feelings. Part of me is relieved to be free of the hundreds and hundreds of hours of work involved. It's not as if being a walk-on coach is a money maker. I figured out once that it comes to less than two dollars per hour. I did better than that in the sugar-beet fields in North Dakota when I was in high school. And that doesn't even count the time outside of practice spent thinking about basketball. As virtually every basketball coach knows, basketball tends to dominate your consciousness.

Part of me is angry and hurt. It turns out that this decision was made some time ago but I was among the last to hear about it. Now I understand my strange encounter with one of the junior-varsity players I ran into when I first got to Fremont yesterday. When I asked her if she was going to play in summer league, she looked at me like I was a ghost and said something I didn't understand, something like "A decision hasn't been made yet." Later I got it—a decision hadn't been made by *the coach*, and that was no longer me. She knew it, but I was still in the dark.

Part of me is embarrassed at having been terminated, for whatever reason. I remember when Jack Vaughn, the former director of the Peace Corps, came to speak at the Business School. I asked him what advice he had for young people starting out in a management career. Jack surprised me: "My advice to anyone who wants to be successful on their own terms is to get fired early and often." His point was that if we are always measuring success by what other people want us to do, we won't make the effort to define success for ourselves. And getting fired makes it pretty much impossible to avoid the struggle to do just that.

A few years ago I did a seminar for the employees of the Score Learning Corporation (now Score @ Kaplan) and a young woman told me about her first failing grade. She was in elementary school and she had never gotten anything less than an A. She worshipped her teacher and was devastated one day after he returned a test to her with an F scrawled across the top of it. She was trying her hardest not to cry right there in front of the entire class when he stunned her by saying "Congratulations." She looked at him like he had lost his mind while he continued "Now you know that you can make a mistake and still survive. Now you can decide for yourself what you want to do and not just do what others want you to do." Pretty heady insight for a grade schooler to assimilate but I guess she did, because she still remembered it after nearly 20 years.

Part of me is glad to have more time to write. I really haven't written much of anything during the last two years. My publisher recently got several calls from people who liked *Positive Coaching* wondering if I had written anything lately. I'm excited about a couple ideas for books on which I did some significant work before I started coaching at Fremont. Now I have no excuse not to get down to work on them.

But that's putting a positive spin on it. Mostly I'm sad, I guess.

No more summer league. No more early-morning workouts. No more three-point shooting contests at the end of practice. No more pre-game visualization exercises. No more waking up in the middle of the night replaying the last game. No more drawing plays on restaurant napkins. No more reviewing videotapes to see how the other team got that wide open shot. No more Creedence Clearwater Revival on the sound system during Saturday practices. No more thrills when Chi slashes to the basket or Natalie dribbles through an entire press all by herself or Sheila handcuffs a player six inches taller with a perfect box-out.

Dave Crawford called to say he was sorry about my losing my job. He tried to cheer me up by mentioning that another walk-on coach at a local high school was bumped right after his team won the CCS baseball title. We only won our league title, so I guess I can't complain too much.

Journal Entry—June 6, 1996, Washington, DC

In DC for the White House Conference on Character Building in a Democratic Society. Had dinner with Andrew Oser of the Joy of Sports Foundation after the Building Character Through Sports Task Force meeting last night. He expressed something I have been struggling to articulate. I told him about losing my coaching job and deciding to

write a book about the experience. I said that even though I didn't believe God reaches down into the world to manipulate events for the
benefit of individual lives, nonetheless this seemed to be a signal that I
am supposed to do something else now. Andrew said he agreed. He
said it perfectly: "When people are truly sincere in trying to understand
what it is they are supposed to do with their lives, the universe will
give them signs."

I liked that a lot. Don't know yet what I'm going to fill those "basketball hours" with, beyond writing this book, but it will be exciting to see
what happens next. I'll keep watching for the signs.

Bibliography

Barnett, William P. and Morton T. Hansen (1996), "The Red Queen in Organizational Evolution," *Strategic Management Journal*, Vol. 17, 139-157.

Berger, P. and T. Luckman (1966). *The Social Construction of Reality*, New York: Doubleday.

Blais, Madeleine (1995), *In These Girls, Hope Is a Muscle*, New York: The Atlantic Monthly Press.

Bloom, Harold (1996), *Omens of Millennium*, New York: Riverhead Books.

Cameron, Julia (1992), *The Artist's Way: A Spiritual Path to Higher Creativity*, New York: G. P. Putnam's Sons.

Carroll, Lewis (1872), *Through the Looking Glass*. Grosset & Dunlap.

Cialdini, Robert (1984), *Influence*, New York: Quill

Cohn, Lowell (1994), *Rough Magic: Bill Walsh's Return to Football*, New York: HarperCollins.

Coles, Robert (1987), *Dorothy Day: A Radical Devotion*, Reading, Massachusetts: Addison-Wesley.

Collins, James C. and Jerry I. Porras (1994), *Built to Last: Successful Habits of Visionary Companies*, New York: HarperBusiness.

Coppola, Eleanor (1979), *Notes: On the Making of "Apocalypse Now,"* New York: Limelight Editions.

Csikszentmihalyi, Mihaly (1990), *Flow: The Psychology of Optimal Experience*, New York: HarperCollins.

DeVenzio, Dick (1982), *Stuff! good players should know*, Charlotte, North Carolina: The Fool Court Press.

Donnithorne, Col. Larry R. (Ret.) (1993), *The West Point Way of Leadership*, New York: Currency Doubleday.

Drucker, Peter (1967), *The Effective Executive*, New York: Harper & Row.

Gardner, John W. (1990), *On Leadership,* New York: The Free Press.

Gladwell, Malcolm (1996), "The Tipping Point," *The New Yorker,* June 3, 1996.

Glasser, William (1976), *Positive Addiction,* New York: Harper & Row.

Goldberg, Natalie (1986), *Writing Down the Bones: Freeing the Writer Within,* Boston: Shambhala.

Goldman, William (1973), *The Princess Bride,* New York: Harcourt Brace Jovanovich.

Hayden, Tom (1988), *Reunion,* New York: Random House.

Herzberg, Frederick (1987), "One more time: How do you motivate employees?" *Harvard Business Review,* September-October 1987.

Hilfiker, David, M.D. (1985), *Healing the Wounds: A Physician Looks at His Work,* New York: Penguin.

Hoffer, Richard (1996), "Sitting Bull," *Sports Illustrated,* May 27, 1996.

Irion, Mary Jean (1970), *Yes, World: A Mosaic of Meditation,* New York: Baron.

Jackson, Phil and Hugh Delehanty (1995), *Sacred Hoops: Spiritual Lessons of a Hardwood Warrior,* New York: Hyperion.

Katzenbach, Jon R. and Douglas K. Smith (1993), *The Wisdom of Teams: Creating the High-Performance Organization,* New York: HarperCollins.

La Belle, Jenijoy (1997), "It's impossible to escape regret," *San Jose Mercury News,* January 5, 1997.

Lepper, Geoff (1996), "Loss Drops Paly Girls Into First Place Tie," *Palo Alto Daily News,* February, 2, 1997.

Levine, David (1989), *Life on the Rim: A Year in the Continental Basketball Association,* New York: Macmillan.

Lao-Tzu (1972), *Tao Te Ching,* New York: Random House.

Leonard, George (1991), *Mastery: The Keys to Success and Long-Term Fulfillment,* New York: Plume.

Leonard, George (1974), *The Ultimate Athlete,* Berkeley, California: North Atlantic Books.

Kingston, Maxine Hong (1975), *The Woman Warrior: Memoirs of a Childhood Among Ghosts,* New York: Vintage.

Maclean, Norman (1992), *Young Men and Fire,* Chicago: University of Chicago Press.

Matthiessen, Peter (1975), *Far Tortuga,* New York: Vintage.

Negroponte, Nicholas (1995), *Being Digital,* New York: Vintage.

Nerenberg, Nancy R. (1994), "The Woman Warrior," *San Jose Mercury News West Magazine,* July 31, 1994.

North, Douglass, (1987) "Institutions and Economic Growth: An Historic Introduction."

Peters, Tom (1992), *Liberation Management: Necessary Disorganization for the Nanosecond Nineties,* New York: Fawcett Columbine.

Pipher, Mary (1994), *Reviving Ophelia: Saving the Lives of Adolescent Girls,* New York: Ballantine.

Reps, Paul (1958), *Zen Flesh Zen Bones,* Rutland, Vermont: C.E. Tuttle.

Rodgers, T. J. and William Taylor and Rick Foreman (1993), *No Excuses Management: Proven Systems for Starting Fast, Growing Quickly, and Surviving Hard Times,* New York: Doubleday.

Rudolph, Susanne and Lloyd I. Rudolph (1967), *Gandhi: The Traditional Roots of Charisma,* Chicago: University of Chicago Press.

Senge, Peter M. (1990), *The Fifth Discipline: The Art and Practice of The Learning Organization,* New York: Doubleday Currency.

Spence, Jonathan (1983), *The Memory Palace of Matteo Ricci,* New York: Penguin.

Tan, Amy (1995), *The Hundred Secret Senses,* New York: G.P. Putnam's Sons.

Thompson, Jim (1996), "The 'visualization' of Eleanor Roosevelt," *San Francisco Examiner,* September 24, 1996.

Thompson, Jim (1995), *Positive Coaching: Building Character and Self-Esteem Through Sports,* Portola Valley, California: Warde Publishers.

Vaill, Peter B. (1989), *Managing as a Performing Art,* San Francisco: Jossey-Bass.

Walsh, Bill with Glenn Dickey (1990), *Building a Champion,* New York: St. Martin's Press.

Weick, Karl (1996), "Prepare Your Organization to Fight Fires," *Harvard Business Review,* May-June 1996, p. 143-148.

Welty, Eudora (1980), *The Collected Stories of Eudora Welty,* New York: Harcourt Brace Jovanovich.

Wills, Garry (1994), *Certain Trumpets: The Call of Leaders,* New York: Simon & Schuster.

Wills, Garry (1994), "What Makes a Good Leader?" *The Atlantic Monthly,* April 1994.

Young, Andrew (1996), *An Easy Burden: The Civil Rights Movement and the Transformation of America,* New York: HarperCollins.

Index

The Positive Coaching Alliance

Dear Reader:

For more than 10 years I have been working to improve the sports experience of young athletes. Both *Positive Coaching* and *Shooting in the Dark* grew out of this effort.

Now I am starting an organization that I hope will help to ignite a movement to transform youth sports so that sports can transform youth.

The **Positive Coaching Alliance** is dedicated to making youth sports an educational, character-building experience that will help our children become successful, self-reliant adults who contribute to our communities. The **Alliance** is made up of coaches, parents, athletes, youth sports organizations and other supporters who share this commitment.

If you want to join me in creating a movement to change youth sports, I welcome your support.

To add your name to the **Positive Coaching Alliance** mailing list, write c/o

> Positive Coaching Alliance
> P. O. Box 9851
> San Jose, CA   95157

or send e-mail to   pca@CharityWeb.net.

Please include your name, address, phone number, fax, and e-mail (all the various ways you can be reached). When the **Alliance** is up and running, we'll be in touch with you. In the meantime you can also check the **Alliance** out on the web at www.CharityWeb.net.

> All the best,
> Jim Thompson